SAINT PAUL

THE FIRST 150 YEARS

Virginia Brainard Kunz

Research: Jane McClure

D1410967

Published by
The Saint Paul Foundation, Inc., in celebration of the
150th Anniversary of the Naming of St. Paul

ACKNOWLEDGMENTS

Few books are ever the work of one person, and this new history of St. Paul is no exception, interwoven as it is with the stories of the people of diverse backgrounds and heritages who played a role in that history. Because of the many complex threads woven through the tapestry of this community, this was, in some respects, a difficult book to write. The task, however, was greatly eased by the support of The Saint Paul Foundation and its staff, who share a lively interest in the history of the community the Foundation serves, as well as the need to understand the roots of the community's cultural diversity.

It was Paul Verret, the Foundation's president, and St. Paul Mayor James Scheibel who began the planning for a celebration of the 150th anniversary of the naming of St. Paul, an event that accompanied the dedication of the Chapel of St. Paul on November 1, 1841. They felt that a new history should be written that would not just trace the march of those years, but would, as well, explore the history of those people who were here first, and of those who followed them.

Dozens of people have taken part in this endeavor. In addition to Paul Verret, Jean Hart, Jane Clements, Dave McDonell, Chris Vitek and other Foundation staff members, I am indebted to the members of the Steering Committee — community leaders who were called together by the Foundation and the mayor to oversee the anniversary celebration in the fall of 1991. Steering Committee members include Mayor Scheibel, honorary chair; Thomas W. McKeown, chair; Paul A. Verret, vice chair; Richard Anfang; Eustolio Benavides III; Dorothea J. Burns; Charmaine S. Chapman; Norbert J. Conzemius; Patrick J. Donovan; Thomas A. Duke; William S. Fallon; Paul Farrell; Phil Fitzpatrick; Curman L. Gaines; Richard Getchell; Aida Gonzalez-Mori; Richard G. Hadley; Daniel J. Hoisington; Jennie Lightfoot Hutcheson; Loeung Khi; Thomas W. Kingston; Judith Kishel; Katherine V. Lilly; James Midtbo; Jim Mullin; Stacy Offner; Anita M. Pampusch; Robert Piram; John Poupart; John R. Roach; A. William Sands, Jr.; Jan Smaby; and Padee Yang. Their interest in the progress of the book and their suggestions as to material to include were enormously helpful.

Another group of community leaders contributed their time and talent to the writing of this manuscript and the production of the book. They are the members of the St. Paul History Sub-committee: Charlton Dietz, William S. Fallon, Phil Fitzpatrick, Ramona Jones, John M. Lindley, Arthur Mc Watt, Laurie Murphy, Marjorie Neihart, John Poupart and Padee Yang. They cheerfully devoted many hours to committee meetings and to reading through several drafts of the manuscript. Their wise and helpful suggestions have improved it substantially. Two other readers of the manuscript, Ronald M. Hubbs and Frank Marzitelli, drew upon their own knowledge of the community's history, and their direct involvement in that history as community leaders over many years, to contribute other valuable comments and recommendations.

I am indebted beyond measure to Jane McClure, who brought to her skillful research her extensive knowledge of community history. This book would not have been possible without her help. A special thanks must go, also, to Sandra Hibbard for her thoughtful editing of the manuscript. Cynthia Hill and Sandy Rummel sifted patiently through numerous suggestions to develop the design for the book, and the result speaks for itself as testimony to their talent. But in the last analysis, all credit must go to the leadership, public and private, of St. Paul and their enlightened understanding of the need for a community to know its past.

V.B.K.

CONTENTS

ACKNOWLEDGMENTS   iii

PREFACE   vi

Part I   1
UNDER SIX FLAGS
1800 - 1840

Part II   15
RUSH TO SETTLEMENT
1840 - 1880

Part III   46
COMING OF AGE
1880 - 1920

Part IV   70
DECADES OF CHANGE
1920 - 1950

Part V   90
A COMMUNITY IN TRANSITION
1950 - 1990

Sources:
READ MORE ABOUT   110
ST. PAUL'S HISTORY

INDEX   114

PHOTO CREDITS   120

PREFACE

Before histories were printed, people learned about their roots and heritage through storytellers who passed their tales from generation to generation. These histories were mostly about people: sometimes individuals — heroes and villains — sometimes families or groups of families.

This new history of St. Paul is about people: people who were here before written histories were recorded and people who came here from other parts of the world in the nineteenth and twentieth centuries.

As generations of these people built this community, they struggled to maintain their roots and individual heritage, while working together — most of the time — to create better lives for themselves and their children.

This history celebrates their diverse roots and recognizes their accomplishments.

The lesson of this story is instructive today. St. Paul has a rich, diverse community — but the tapestry includes new families of many different colors, who came here from other regions of the United States or different continents.

A history of our community's diversity reminds us that the stresses, strains and even conflicts present opportunities, not obstacles, to building a community. We can value and celebrate our differences while focusing on common goals of a high quality of life for all citizens.

As we celebrate the 150th anniversary of the naming of our city, we're sure you'll enjoy and learn from Virginia Kunz's new stories of St. Paul.

James Scheibel
Honorary Chair of the
150th Anniversary
Steering Committee
Mayor
City of St. Paul

Thomas W. McKeown
Chair of the
150th Anniversary
Steering Committee
Executive Vice President
The St. Paul Companies

Youngsters enjoyed a downtown toboggan slide during the St. Paul Winter Carnival.
Ice slides and flooded streets for skating were Carnival features in the 1950s and 1960s.

Lieutenant Zebulon Pike's explorations are recalled by this expedition map, which shows the region around the site of St. Paul. Pike's mission was to find the source of the Mississippi, to explore the topography, and to find sites for forts — including Fort Snelling — to block British fur trade routes.

UNDER SIX FLAGS
1800 – 1840

The river current flowing southward would have nudged the boats toward the east bank of the Mississippi as Lieutenant Zebulon Pike and his little band approached the great curve where the river swung toward the southwest.

Spread out before him was the flat plain on the west of the river. To the east were the astonishingly white bluffs that to this day are familiar to people whose homes fill the Mississippi's valley at St. Paul. The bluffs, rising eighty feet above the river, were bracketed by clefts a mile or so apart. Streams flowing through the clefts suggested convenient landing places, but the young army officer led his men farther upstream to the mouth of the Minnesota (then known as St. Peter's) River. There they landed on an island that still bears Pike's name.

Pike had been sent north from St. Louis in 1805 to explore the headwaters of the Mississippi. His journey was part of the Lewis and Clark expedition that ascended the Missouri and reached the Pacific. The purpose

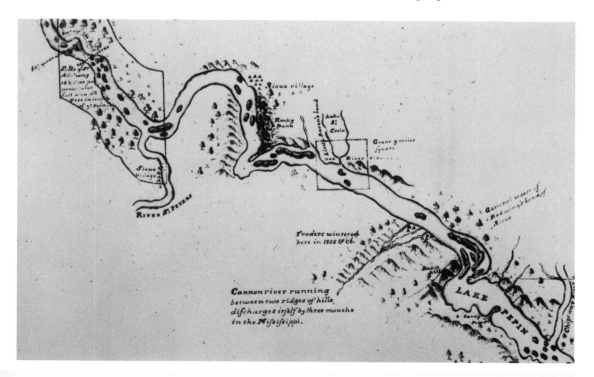

of both expeditions was to examine Thomas Jefferson's 1803 purchase of Louisiana, a vast 857,000-square-mile tract of land that spread west from New Orleans and north to the hazy boundary — established in 1783 at the end of the American Revolution — between British and American possessions.

Jefferson wanted Pike to follow the Mississippi to its source, examine the geography and resources of the area, record the "population and residence" of the Native Americans, and seek sites for military posts. It was late September in 1805 when Pike landed his force of twenty men on Pike Island. On September 23, he met in council with 150 Dakota warriors led by Little Crow, grandfather of the man who would lead the Dakota Conflict of 1862.

In the treaty signed by Pike and by "Le Petit Corbeau" (Little Crow) and Way Aga Enagee, who represented the Dakota, the United States government acquired 155,520 acres of land. In return, the government offered $200 in presents, sixty gallons of whiskey, and a sum of $2,000. The money was not paid until 1819, and then it was valued in goods rather than gold. The estimated cost to the government for the purchase was $1.28 an acre.

Pike knew he hadn't ventured into unknown territory or an uninhabited wilderness. The flags of five other nations had flown over the region before the arrival of the Americans with Pike and his men: the banners of the Native Americans who were the original inhabitants of the region, the lions of Spain, the *fleur de lys* of the French monarchy, the tricolor of the French republic, and the Union Jack of Great Britain. While this region was claimed through exploration or conquest by governments thousands of miles away, it had belonged for centuries to the Ojibway (Chippewa) and Dakota (Sioux). Both tribes had joined — first with the French, then with the British — in the rich fur trade.

At a time when the first Europeans were arriving along the eastern seaboard during the seventeenth century, the Dakota nation had moved north from its original home in the Midwest. From the "upper country" the Dakota controlled a vast domain extending from Michigan to the "shining mountains." Their chief village in what is now Minnesota was Kathio at Mille Lacs.

By the middle of the eighteenth century, the Dakota had been pushed out of their northern forests and onto the southern Minnesota prairies by the Ojibway. People of Algonquian stock who had moved west from their homeland near the mouth of the St. Lawrence River, the Ojibway were allies of the explorer and fur trader, Sieur Du Luth, and served as middlemen between the French and the Dakota. At first the Dakota allowed the Ojibway to use Dakota hunting and fishing grounds. However, as the Ojibway pushed the Dakota south and west, what had been a peaceful relationship degenerated into a long conflict between the two tribes for control of the northern forests. The enmity the struggle aroused eventually spilled over into pioneer St. Paul.

The Dakota had lived in the area for many years before the first white settlers arrived.

While the Dakota bands did not at first establish permanent villages along the Mississippi and Minnesota rivers near present-day St. Paul, the region was a vast trading area and a frequent halting place for their war and hunting parties. The Dakota presence still marks modern-day St. Paul. Snelling Avenue, West Seventh Street, and even Interstate 94 follow what once were Dakota trails. Mendota, at the junction of the two rivers, was a sacred meeting place where the bands held ceremonies and councils, as was the mysterious Red Rock at what is now Newport, down the Mississippi from St. Paul. The region lying between the Mississippi and St. Croix rivers served as a rich "pantry," teeming with game and fish and berries that supported the Dakota.

The diversity of cultures and of people who played a role in St. Paul's history begins with these Native Americans who first dwelt in the region. The earliest Europeans, such as Daniel Greysolon, Sieur Du Luth, were just passing through. In June, 1680, Du Luth paddled near Ramsey County's fringes as he journeyed down the St. Croix to the Mississippi. That same spring, Father Louis Hennepin, a Frenchman, was captured by a party of Dakota near today's Iowa border. Hennepin was attached to the expedition of Robert Cavelier, Sieur de La Salle, commissioned by Louis XIV to explore the unknown West. Hennepin, two other Frenchmen and their captors probably landed at the little bay at the mouth of Phalen Creek on their way to Kathio, the Dakota headquarters. The next spring, while in the company of a party of Dakota, Father Hennepin discovered and named St. Anthony Falls.

The real European invasion began in the eighteenth century when the French established fur trading posts in the region they had claimed as part of New France, France's North American empire that spread from Canada to the Ohio and Mississippi River valleys. Distracted as they were by events in Europe, the French, however, had neither the money, the men nor the inclination for permanent settlement. The loss of New France to Britain at the end of the French and Indian War of 1763 put an end to the French presence in the Minnesota region for a time.

Jonathan Carver, in his colorful but sometimes fanciful account of his expedition into Minnesota in 1766 and 1767, described meeting three bands of the "Naudowessie" (or Nadowaysioux, an Ojibway term shortened by the French traders to Sioux; the Sioux called themselves Dakota, meaning "friend" or "allies"). Carver encountered the bands near the St. Croix River and noted that these Dakota were called "river bands" or "Mdewakanton" because, he wrote, they lived near the banks of the river. (Mdewakanton

Carver's Cave is named for adventurer Jonathan Carver. His descriptions of Dakota ceremonies held in the cave still captivate readers today.

also meant Spirit Lake Village; and the bands were from one of four tribes of the Santee, or eastern, Dakota.)

In writing of the famous cave that bears his name, Carver suggested that St. Paul was perhaps a "pre-destined capital." It was the custom, he said, for the Dakota people to hold a grand council of all the bands each year at the cave. There they "settle[d] their operations for the ensuing year" and buried the bones of their dead "in the burial-place that stands adjacent to [Carver's cave]."

The Dakota and Ojibway of the region added an interesting footnote to history during the American Revolution. Both were allies of the British. The Dakota chief, Wabasha, and the Ojibway chief, Matchekewis, helped the British recruit 750 Native Americans and traders for an attack on St. Louis. The city was held by the Spanish, who had entered the war on the American side in 1779. Wabasha, commissioned a general in the British army and wearing a British uniform, commanded 200 Santee Sioux warriors. The attack, known as the "coup d'anee," took place May 26, 1780. It was repulsed, and Wabasha and his force retreated to Prairie du Chien. The attack remains the only known involvement in the Revolution by men living in what is now Minnesota.

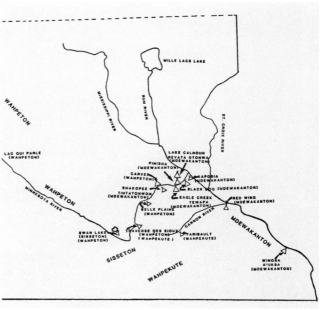

Village locations of the Mdewakanton bands of the Santee or Eastern Dakota Indians in 1834.

By the early nineteenth century, the Mdewakanton bands had established five villages near the junction of the Mississippi and Minnesota rivers: Cloud Man's village at Lake Calhoun; the Black Dog, Good Road and Shakopee communities along the Minnesota River; and Kaposia, located first on the east bank of the Mississippi below Dayton's Bluff and later on the west bank at today's South St. Paul. A map drawn by a government cartographer from Pike's notes of his journey shows a "Sioux village" near the point where Phalen Creek empties into the Mississippi.

The British, who followed the French into the region after 1763, by-passed St. Paul's site to establish such far-flung northern Minnesota posts as Grand Portage, Fond du Lac, Sandy Lake and Leech Lake. Because of Britain's reluctance to withdraw from the territory they had lost to the Americans in the Revolution, the American government began to speculate on the need for a northern military post that would keep an eye on the British.

Lawrence Taliaferro, when he was Indian agent for the region.

It was not until after the War of 1812 that the United States established a post in the region – Fort Snelling, one of a cordon of forts built along the frontier for, according to John C. Calhoun, secretary of war, "the protection of our [fur] trade and the preservation of the peace of the frontier." It was, at that time, the northernmost military post in the United States. With the construction of the fort in the 1820s, the history of St. Paul as a community began.

Arriving as construction of the fort was under way was a man who would be, in the words of historian W. W. Folwell, "the most important and influential civil official on the upper Mississippi." Lawrence Taliaferro, an army officer personally selected by President Monroe to be Indian agent for the region, was a Virginian of Italian ancestry. He was just twenty-five years old when he took up his post. For the next twenty years, Taliaferro operated his Indian agency from a series of log buildings that stood a little to the southeast of Fort Snelling. From there he attempted to protect the Dakota and Ojibway from the machinations of the traders and dampen the bitter warfare between the tribes. He established a "Sioux-Chippewa" line running diagonally from the St. Croix River through Minnesota, passing near present-day St. Cloud and Alexandria, to the Red River. Taliaferro asked the Ojibway bands to stay north of the line and the Dakota to remain south. It was a porous border, however, that failed to keep the two warring nations apart.

Although stuffy, self-righteous and occasionally quarrelsome, Taliaferro also was honest and incorruptible. "It is to his credit," wrote Folwell, "that he was cordially hated by all who could neither bribe nor frighten him to connive at law breaking to the harm of the Indians."

Inevitably, the protection Fort Snelling offered the region attracted civilians known as "squatters" — illegal settlers on land reserved for the military. In 1811, the Scottish Earl of Selkirk, who owned controlling interest in the Hudson's Bay Company, established the Selkirk colony near Fort Garry — today's Winnipeg, Manitoba. He based his colony on a somewhat Utopian dream of providing homes for poor European immigrants who would grow food for his fur traders. In 1821, Selkirk's agents in Europe recruited a group of 165 Swiss mechanics and tradesmen, which included watch and clock makers, pastry cooks, and musicians. These immigrants settled down at Fort Garry along with a number of French and *metis* (mixed blood) fur traders and their families. The colonists soon found that conditions were far from Utopian. They were bedeviled by drought, excessive cold, plagues of mice and grasshoppers, and flooding of the Red River.

Taking the well-traveled route from Fort Garry to the mouth of the Minnesota River, a group of refugees from the colony arrived at Fort Snelling in 1821. Colonel Josiah Snelling, commandant at the fort, allowed them to use Camp Cold Water, the abandoned barracks that had housed the soldiers who built the fort. The old camp was north of the fort on a bluff above the west bank of the Mississippi. Some opened small farms; others continued to work in the fur trade.

Throughout the next fifteen years, they were joined by a steady stream of disheartened refugees from Fort Garry. Among them were Abraham Perry (or Perret) and Benjamin Gervais — each of whom would play a part in St. Paul's early history. There were other illegal settlers on

Fort Snelling, as it appeared in 1850. The fort was begun in 1819 as the northernmost of a chain of frontier outposts. This painting was incorrectly believed to be the work of Seth Eastman. Sergeant Edward K. Thomas, who was at the fort from 1849 to 1851, was the artist.

Seth Eastman did use the Fort Snelling site frequently in his sketches and paintings. Eastman was an Army officer and four-time commandant at the fort. He served as a brigadier general in the Civil War.

military property — voyageurs who had retired from the fur trade, and soldiers who had been discharged from the army and who built cabins along the Mississippi opposite the fort.

All might have gone well in this settlement, had not relations between the military and the civilians become strained. The post command was growing increasingly concerned about dwindling supplies of forage and fuel, since both soldiers and settlers pastured cattle and cut timber on the same land. A more serious and emotional issue concerned the sale of whiskey to soldiers and Indians by the retired fur traders living illegally in their cabins in what is now Highland Park.

"Since the middle of winter," the fort's surgeon wrote in April, 1839, "we have been completely inundated with ardent spirits, and consequently the most beastly scenes of intoxication among the soldiers of this garrison and the Indians in its vicinity, which no doubt will add many cases to our sick list...." The problem grew to such proportions that on June 3, 1839, forty-seven soldiers were in the guardhouse after a riotous spree in a dram shop across the river.

It is perhaps not surprising that liquor was a problem. Life at the frontier post, at best, was lonely and monotonous. When the long day of labor and drill ended, there was little for the men to do. The handful of white women at the fort were, for the most part, officers' wives. Some enlisted men had been allowed to bring their wives, and they often worked as cooks, laundresses and servants in the officers' quarters. Social events, such as balls and amateur theatrics, enlivened the long winter for the officers, although with only fireplaces for warmth, their wives often shivered in their low-cut gowns. (Stoves didn't arrive until the 1830s.)

As Fort Snelling attracted illegal settlers, it also offered protection to another group of civilians: the missionaries who often were in the forefront of efforts to explore and settle new lands. Samuel and Gideon Pond and the Reverend Jedediah Stevens were with Chief Cloudman's band at Lake Calhoun. The Reverend Alfred Brunson was at Kaposia, which at this time was still on the east bank of the Mississippi below Dayton's Bluff.

An interesting picture has been left of the Kaposia of this time period. Little Crow's band was small — approximately 200 men, women and children, including some seventy warriors. Their homes were comfortable, with palisaded walls of tamarack poles and roofs of brush covered with bark. Little Crow's dwelling was large — thirty feet long with two rooms — and the lodges were set up against the bluff for protection.

Both Reverend Brunson and Lawrence Taliaferro figured in the early history of the African Americans in the St. Paul area. Taliaferro played a part in the famous Dred Scott case. In the Missouri Compromise of 1820, Congress had prohibited slavery in the northern territory of the Louisiana Purchase, which included Minnesota. Nevertheless, Taliaferro and Dr. John Emerson, Fort Snelling's surgeon, owned slaves. In 1836, Emerson brought Dred Scott to Fort Snelling from Missouri, a slave state. While at the fort, Scott married another slave named Harriet, who was originally owned by Taliaferro and sold by Taliaferro to Emerson. When Emerson was transferred back to Missouri, he took Dred and Harriet Scott with him. Although he was back in a slave state, Scott sued for his freedom in 1846, on the grounds that his residence in Minnesota and several other free territories had made him a free man.

The case reached the United States Supreme Court. In ruling that it had no jurisdiction in the case, the Court, in effect, decided that Scott remained a slave. The landmark decision in the Scott case aroused violent public reaction. The Court also ruled that Scott, as a slave, was not a citizen who could bring suit for his freedom and that the United States Congress had no power to prohibit slavery in United States territories. The decision was an important factor that led to the Civil War.

Brunson was involved in the lesser known story of James Thompson, the servant of an officer at Prairie du Chien. Thompson, who had earlier been stationed at Fort Snelling with his owner, had married a Dakota woman and was fluent in her language. Brunson, needing an interpreter, bought Thompson, set him free, and brought him to Kaposia in 1837. There, Thompson worked with Brunson in ministering to the Dakota in their village. A few years later, Thompson joined the little band of settlers who were the first residents of St. Paul.

Dred Scott, whose quest for freedom led to a landmark court decision.

Throughout the 1830s and 1840s, Fort Snelling was a hardship post. Its officers were for the most part veterans of the War of 1812 or graduates of West Point. One West Point graduate, Zachary Taylor, fort commandant between 1828 and 1829, later became the only president of the United States to live for any time in Minnesota.

The fort's enlisted men represented a cultural mix of German and Irish immigrants and New England Yankees, some of whom would also help settle St. Paul. In a poignant letter to his wife back in Detroit, Private Gustavus Otto, an immigrant from Bavaria, described the day-to-day struggle of life on the frontier in the late 1840s:

Zachary Taylor, Fort Snelling commandant, 1828-29.

"The winters are very cold here...We are in thick stone buildings and each two men have woolen blankets...and yet we had to make a fire in the middle of the night in order not to freeze. We sometimes had to relieve one another to guard every quarter or one-half hour. I have then like many others frozen my ears, nose and face, but God gave me his assistance."

Some of Otto's fellow soldiers among the Irish were already living in the small settlement that became St. Paul. In 1837, the United States government negotiated treaties with the Dakota, who ceded Dakota lands from the St. Croix River on the east, to today's Crow Wing and Aitken counties on the north and to the Mississippi on the west — the very region that once, in a sense, had been the Dakotas' "pantry." While the negotiations were the result of the inevitable pressure to open more land to white settlement, the Dakota themselves were becoming increasingly desperate. Under the pressures of population growth, their game was disappearing, and "white men's sicknesses" were visiting their villages.

The 1837 treaties promised the Dakota annuities in money, goods and provisions; but even before payment began, cabins were going up along the Mississippi. For the Selkirk settlers and others living around the fort, the treaties that opened up new land to settlement also signaled expulsion from the military reservation.

A survey of the military reservation in October, 1837, showed eighty-two inhabitants at Camp Cold Water, seventy-five at Mendota and five or six others on the east side of the Mississippi, including Joseph and Amabel Turpin, Joseph Rondo, Francis Desire and Donald McDonald. A former fur trader, McDonald claimed the land along the Mississippi between present-day Marshall Avenue and Highway 94, opened a dram shop and later sold out to Stephen Desnoyer for a "barrel of whiskey and two Indian guns."

The survey extended the reservation's boundaries down the river, and the squatters were told they would have to move. They protested their eviction, but to no avail. In 1838, they moved down the Mississippi and resettled around Fountain Cave, on the east bank of the river between present-day Barton and Randolph streets, a location they believed to be just outside the reservation boundaries.

Among the settlers was Abraham Perry, a Swiss watchmaker who had emigrated to the Selkirk colony in 1820 and who joined the great exodus to Fort Snelling after a disastrous flood in 1826. Settling at Camp Cold Water, Perry opened a farm and prospered. At one time he was reported to have owned more cattle than anyone else in the region.

Benjamin and Pierre Gervais, who were French Canadians and had arrived at the Cold Water settlement in the mid-1820s, also made claims at Fountain Cave. Both were fur traders who had lived for some years with the Selkirk Colony. Benjamin worked for the Hudson's Bay Company and Pierre for the American Fur Company at Mendota.

Fountain Cave, as it appeared on an 1875 postcard. The cave is one of many that figure in St. Paul's history. It is most often remembered as "Pig's Eye" Parrant's first home in what is now St. Paul.

Already in residence at Fountain Cave was the infamous but colorful Pierre "Pig's Eye" Parrant, whom historian J. Fletcher Williams nominated as "the Romulus of our future city." A French Canadian voyageur who arrived in Mendota in 1832, Parrant apparently caused Lawrence Taliaferro no end of trouble. In 1835, the Indian agent noted in his journal that he had "ordered Pierre Parrant, a foreigner, prohibited from the trade, not to enter the Indian country in any capacity." Parrant's misdeeds (whatever they were) apparently were serious; and his personal appearance also did nothing to inspire confidence. Parrant was about sixty years of age at this time. He was described as a coarse, ill-looking, low-browed fellow. He had a blind eye that, according to Williams, was marble-hued and crooked, with a sinister white ring glaring around the pupil, giving a kind of piggish expression to his "sodden, low features."

Charles and Angelina Perry. He was the last living survivor of the ill-fated Selkirk Colony.

In the spring of 1838, Parrant staked a claim near Perry's. He proposed to set himself up in the whiskey business. His judgment was sound. A sergeant at Fort Snelling reportedly had paid $80, one cold winter night, for a gallon of whiskey that very likely cost the seller a dollar. Parrant also chose his location well. He built his hovel in the secluded and lonely gorge that sheltered the mouth of a clear little stream flowing out of Fountain Cave into the Mississippi. Customers could paddle to his door and steamboats could stop to unload his supplies.

In July of 1838, three discharged soldiers from Fort Snelling — Edward Phelan, John Hays and William Evans, all natives of Ireland — filed claims to land downstream from the Fountain Cave settlement. Evans selected a spot on Dayton's Bluff. The tract of land Phelan and Hays selected for their claims extended along the river and the bluffs from present-day Eagle Street on the west to today's Minnesota Street on the east. With the help of James Thompson, Phelan and Hays built a log house half-way down the bluff near Eagle Street. Phelan and Hays seem to have been the first settlers in what is now downtown St. Paul.

As illicit liquor continued to be a problem for the command at Fort Snelling, the military reservation's lines were extended once again — as far as today's Seven Corners. Since the new boundaries included the Fountain Cave community, its residents once again were ordered to move. The settlers appealed, again to no avail. Then they simply refused to leave. In May, 1840, a military force from Fort Snelling drove them from their homes and destroyed their cabins.

Wearily, they collected their belongings and moved into what is now downtown St. Paul. There, the permanent settlement of St. Paul took root.

It was an auspicious beginning. The site was, to all intents and purposes, the head of navigation on the upper Mississippi. The clefts in the eighty-foot bluffs, sighted by Pike thirty-five years earlier, created the two landing places that still exist as the Lower Landing or levee — called Lambert's Landing today — at the foot of Jackson Street and the Upper Landing or levee at the foot of Chestnut Street.

Parrant, again, had preceded the other settlers. Having lost his Fountain Cave claim, he acquired another that extended from Minnesota to Jackson streets. Near the foot of what is now Robert Street and on a slight rise of ground, he built another hovel where he continued to sell liquor. The little settlement was at first nameless, but due to the presence of the ubiquitous Parrant, that soon changed. Edmund Brissett, a young French Canadian who was working at odd jobs in the village, told J. Fletcher Williams how he named the community in the course of needing a place at which to date a letter. He was stopping, at the time, at Parrant's tavern.

"I looked up inquiringly at Parrant," he recalled, "and, seeing his old crooked eye scowling at me, it suddenly popped into my head to date it at

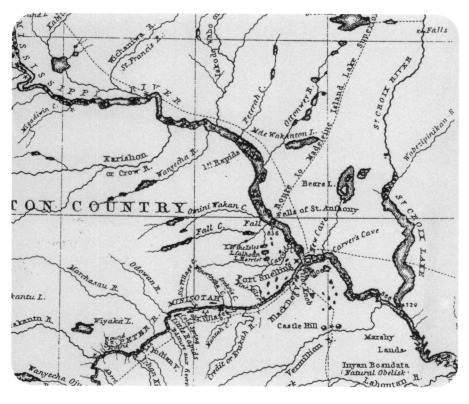

This portion of Joseph Nicollet's map of the "Hydrographic Basin of the Upper Mississippi" includes many details of the region around St. Paul.

Pig's Eye, feeling sure that the place would be recognized, as Parrant was well known along the river. In a little while an answer was safely received, directed to me at Pig's Eye. I told the joke to some of the boys and they made lots of fun of Parrant. He was very mad, and threatened to lick me, but never tried to execute it."

In 1844, Parrant sold his claim at the Lower Landing to Benjamin Gervais and moved to the Grand Marais, the alluvial bottom land along the Mississippi below St. Paul. He stayed there only a few months before losing that claim. He started for Sault Ste. Marie, but he never arrived. According to Williams, he died before reaching Lake Superior "of a disease resulting from his own vices." His name, however, has remained attached to Pig's Eye Lake, the area of his last claim.

PART II

RUSH TO SETTLEMENT
1840 – 1880

As 1840 dawned, nine cabins were strewn along the bluffs between the Lower and the Upper Landings. The river bottom was studded with ancient, stately trees. Stands of cedar and tamarack followed the base of the Summit Avenue hill and a dense forest of elms surrounded the Upper Landing.

A bog extended from present-day Washington Street and Kellogg Boulevard north past Assumption Church and west to Seven Corners. A stream ran through this area and drained into the Mississippi at the Upper Landing. At Cedar and Tenth streets, another stream tumbled over a ledge to create a small waterfall. The falls drained into a sizable lake at Eighth and Robert, and the stream then ran through a deep ravine along Jackson Street and into the river.

The little settlement already had seen its first birth, its first marriage, its first mystery and its first death — by murder. On a September morning in 1839, John Hays' body was found in the river below Carver's Cave, his head bashed in, apparently by violent blows.

Phelan, Hays' claim partner, was immediately arrested and hauled off to Prairie du Chien, 300 miles away, to await trial. The evidence was circumstantial. Hays, regarded as a decent sort of man, had saved some money. Phelan, who was penniless, had a reputation for cruelty and earlier

In 1851, downtown St. Paul was a small collection of log cabins, stores, a stable, a tavern and a church.

Benjamin Gervais, pioneer farmer, with his wife.

had threatened Hays. After a hearing, Phelan was released for lack of evidence. (Some years later a Dakota Indian, Dowah the Singer, was fatally wounded during the battle of Kaposia, and confessed on his deathbed that he had killed Hays.)

Phelan returned to St. Paul and made a new claim near the site of the Hamm Brewery and on the creek that bears his name. Still troublesome, he was indicted in 1850 for perjury (unrelated to the Hays murder) by the first grand jury to sit in Ramsey County. Phelan fled before he could be arrested. He joined the trek to the California gold fields, but came to a violent end while crossing the plains.

A mystery that was the talk of the village for some months surrounded a man known simply as "Johnson." He arrived one day seemingly out of nowhere with a woman and a child. He was mild-mannered and fashionably dressed — definitely not a rough frontiersman; the woman with him, who was presumed to be his wife, was young and refined. They appeared to be "very much attached to each other," as the old accounts stated rather primly.

Rumors flew — he was a criminal; a counterfeiter; he had run off with another man's wife. Then one day Johnson committed the unpardonable sin on the frontier. He turned away a traveler from his door. Asked to leave the village or suffer the penalty of being reported to the authorities at Fort Snelling, he took the woman and the child and vanished as mysteriously as he had arrived, and for 150 years the mystery has remained unsolved.

Rose Ann Perry Clewett and her son. Rose Ann's marriage to James Clewett was the first wedding in St. Paul.

The first marriage introduced another element of high romance into the hamlet. James R. Clewett, a young Englishman drawn to the west by a love of adventure, had come to Mendota several years earlier as an employee of the American Fur Company. Mendota — at that time a predominantly French settlement — was the social center of the region. The dances held there to enliven the long winter months were alight with the Gallic love of life and color. With all the gallantry of their French ancestry, the men dressed for these occasions in black coats and trousers, fine cambric shirts and brilliant woven sashes. They were tireless dancers, as Denis Cherrier, a fiddler who furnished the music, remembered long afterward.

It was at one of these dances that Clewett first saw Rose Perry, the young daughter of Abraham Perry. Clewett went home with the Perrys that night and stayed there until Rose agreed to marry him. They were married on April 9, 1839, by the Reverend J. W. Pond, a Methodist missionary at Kaposia.

In September, 1839, the first white child in the settlement, Basil Gervais, was born. Also referred to as Bazil or Bazille in early histories, he was the child of Benjamin Gervais and his wife, Genevieve Larans, a native of Berthier, Canada.

With Protestant missions already open at Kaposia, Red Rock and Lake Harriet, and the community that included Mendota, Fort Snelling and the site of St. Paul, the Catholics at Dubuque began to see the need to assign a priest to the region. They sent the newly-ordained twenty-nine-year-old Frenchman, Lucien Galtier. He arrived at Mendota in the spring of 1840.

Born in France in 1811, Galtier was studying theology there when Bishop Mathias Loras of Dubuque arrived in Europe. The bishop was seeking laborers for his vast vineyard in the heart of America, and Galtier was among the missionaries he recruited. Father Galtier's assignment was to minister to approximately 185 Catholics, including the French from Canada as well as others at Mendota and the settlement called Pig's Eye. Actually, Galtier was out of his jurisdiction at Pig's Eye. The little community was east of the Mississippi within the Territory of Wisconsin and, therefore, was the responsibility of the bishop of Detroit. No matter. There was no other priest within hundreds of miles.

Galtier soon cast about for a site for a chapel. Years later, in 1864, he wrote a firsthand account of the building of the Chapel of St. Paul and the naming of the settlement for the chapel.

Father Lucien Galtier, who gave St. Paul its name.

"Three different points were offered," he wrote, "one called La Point Basse, or Point Le Claire [the point down the river still known as Pig's Eye], but I objected because that locality was exposed to inundation. The idea of building a church which might at any day be swept down the river to Saint Louis, did not please me.

"Two miles and a half further up on his elevated claim [now the southern point of Dayton's Bluff], Mr. Charles Mousseau offered me an acre of his ground, but the place did not suit my purpose. I was truly looking ahead, thinking of the future as well as the present.

Steamboats could not stop there; the bank was too steep, the place on the summit of the hill too restricted; communication difficult with the other parts of the settlement up and down the river.

"After mature reflection, I resolved to put up the church at the nearest possible point to [Fountain] Cave, because it would be more convenient for me to cross the river there, when coming from Saint Peter's [Mendota], and because, also, it would be the nearest point to the head of navigation, outside of the [Fort Snelling Military] Reservation line.

"Mr. B. Gervais and Mr. Vetal Guerin, two good quiet farmers, had the only spot that appeared likely to answer the purpose. They consented to give me jointly the ground necessary for a church site, a garden and a small graveyard. I accepted the extreme eastern part of Mr. Vetal's claim, and the extreme west of Mr. Gervais'.

"Accordingly, in 1841, in the month of October, logs were prepared and a church erected, so poor that it would well remind one of the stable at Bethlehem. It was destined, however, to be the nucleus of a great city. On the 1st day of November, in that same year, I blessed the new basilica, and dedicated it to 'Saint Paul, the apostle of nations.' I expressed a wish, at that time, that the settlement would be known by the same name and my desire was obtained.

"I had previously to this time fixed my residence at Saint Peter's, and as the name of Paul is generally connected with that of Peter, and the gentiles being well represented in the persons of the Indians, I called it Saint Paul. The name 'Saint Paul,' applied to a town or city, seemed appropriate. The monosyllable is short, sounds well, and is understood by all denominations of Christians.

"When Mr. Vetal Guerin was married, I published the bans as being those of a resident of 'Saint Paul.' A Mr. Jackson put up a store, and a grocery was opened at the foot of the Gervais claim. This soon brought steamboats to land there. Thenceforth the place was known as 'Saint Paul Landing,' and, later on, as 'Saint Paul.'"

Nearly sixty years later, Isaac LaBissonniere, who at the age of eighteen had helped build the chapel, remembered its construction. He was one of the first eight men who volunteered to do the work. He recalled that his father served "by general consent" as general superintendent of the project. Others among them were Benjamin and Pierre Gervais, Pierre and Charles Bottineau, Francois Morin and Vetal Guerin — a constellation of French names.

"The ground selected for the site...was thinly covered with groves of red oak and white oak," Isaac LaBissonniere recalled. *"Where the cathedral stands [near Sixth and Wabasha] was then a tamarack swamp. The logs for the chapel were cut on the spot and the tamarack swamp in the rear was made to contribute rafters and roof pieces. We had poor building tools in those days and our work was not beautifully finished.*

"The logs, rough and undressed, prepared merely by the ax, were made secure by wooden pins. The roof was made of steeply slanting bark-covered slabs, donated by a millowner of Stillwater. The slabs were carried to St. Paul by a steamboat, the captain accepting in payment a few days' service of one of the men. These slabs were landed at Jackson Street and were drawn up the hill by hand with ropes. The slabs were likewise put to good use in the construction of the floor and of the benches.

"So poor it would well remind one of the stable of Bethlehem," was how Father Galtier later described the Chapel of St. Paul.

"The chapel, as I remember it, was about twenty-five feet long, eighteen feet wide, and ten feet high. It had a single window on each side and it faced the river. It was completed in a few days, and could not have represented an expenditure in labor value of more than $65."

On All Saints Day, November 1, 1841, Father Galtier dedicated the little chapel. It was located on Bench Street, now Second Street, between Cedar and Minnesota streets. The "small graveyard" Galtier mentions was near what later became Third (now Kellogg Boulevard) and Minnesota streets. Galtier was transferred to Iowa three years later and Father Augustine Ravoux succeeded him. In 1847, Ravoux extended the rear of the chapel to forty-five feet and added a small belfry to house the bell of the ARGO, a steamboat that had sunk in the Mississippi.

In 1851, after the diocese of St. Paul had been established and Joseph Cretin named bishop, the humble little bark-roofed log building became the cathedral of the diocese. Three more cathedrals were to follow. Two were built on the square once known throughout St. Paul as the "cathedral block." Bounded by Wabasha and St. Peter, Sixth and Seventh streets, "cathedral block" was on land owned originally by Vetal Guerin, who sold it to Bishop Cretin.

The present cathedral on Selby and Summit avenues was completed in 1915. The vestry of the old chapel was used for a time by the Sisters of St. Joseph as a school. According to J. Fletcher Williams, the little building became dilapidated and was dismantled in about 1856. Its logs were carefully numbered and later hauled up St. Anthony hill to the site purchased for St. Joseph's Academy. The intention was to rebuild the chapel and preserve it as a relic. No one told the men who were working on the construction of the Academy in 1863, what the logs were for; they burned them to warm hands and coffee. Two fragments survived and were used to make gavels for the St. Paul Cathedral and the Minnesota Historical Society. By 1907, these, too, had disappeared.

If for no other reason, Galtier would go down in history as the man who effected St. Paul's escape from the humiliation of being known up and down the river as Pig's Eye. "No town — not even one having all the natural advantages possessed by St. Paul — could ever have survived the name of Pig's Eye," historian W. B. Hennessy noted in 1906. "And it should be remembered to Father Galtier, of blessed memory, that not the least of his deeds on behalf of posterity was the rescuing of St. Paul from the swinish appellation it was given at the hands of Edmund Brissett."

The newly-christened village of St. Paul was a French-speaking community. The men who built the huts huddled on the bluff above the steamboat landing were, for the most part, rough men of the forests and streams. They were fur traders and voyageurs who spent part of the year working for Henry H. Sibley and the American Fur Company at Mendota, and the remaining months farming small plots in St. Paul. Their wives had learned how to endure the hardships of the frontier. Mary Ann Perry, in particular, was an accomplished midwife and much in demand among the women at Fort Snelling. Vetal Guerin, whose cabin stood on the southeast corner of present-day Kellogg Boulevard and Wabasha Street, tended a wheat field where the downtown Radisson Hotel and Victory Memorial Parking Ramp now stand. When he married Adele Perry in 1841, their wedding was a riotous event. Denis Cherrier played his fiddle to the point of exhaustion; and the guests, who included every man, woman and child in the settlement, feasted on deer, prairie chicken, rabbits, fish and tiers of cakes.

Vetal Guerin had moved to Seventh and Wabasha when Robert O. Sweeny sketched Guerin's home in 1852.

The home to which Guerin led his bride was as spartan as the chapel he had helped build. It was typical of the huts of these early settlers. Logs hewn flat and chinked with mud formed the walls, bark made up the roof, and a large fireplace of mud covered part of an end wall. There was a window and a door and a floor of split logs. Furniture consisted of a chest that did double duty as wardrobe and dining table; several stools; and a bed made of poles set against a wall, filled with hay, and covered with a red blanket and a buffalo hide. Adele Guerin traded a shawl for feathers to soften the bed.

By 1845, there were some thirty families, most of them French Canadian, living in cabins scattered from present-day Seven Corners to Lake Phalen. Because it was a predominantly French-speaking community, interpreters often were needed. The French were for the most part from the Selkirk Colony; the Swiss were represented by the Perry family; the Irish by Phelan and William Evans; the Danes by Charles W. W. Borup, fur trader, banker and lumberman; and the African Americans by James Thompson.

In 1849, Thompson contributed 15,000 shingles, 2,000 feet of lumber and considerable money and labor to build the first Methodist church in St. Paul. Erected on Market Street, on the site today of the Saint Paul Hotel, the Market Street Methodist Church served a number of different congregations throughout its years.

W. H. Forbes operated this trading post, the Minnesota Outfit, at Third and Jackson in 1847. Sketch by Robert O. Sweeny.

The Native Americans — particularly the Dakota at Kaposia — were a continuing presence in the village. Among the settlers themselves, the Native Americans were richly represented. Elizabeth Beaulieu, Charles Borup's wife, was the daughter of a French Canadian fur trader and an Ojibway woman. Scott Campbell represented both the Scots through his father, a noted trader named Colin Campbell, and the Native Americans, first through his mother and later through his wife, Margaret, a Menominee. Campbell was a gifted linguist who spoke French, English and a number of Native American tongues. This ability served him well during his twenty-five years as interpreter at the Indian agency at Fort Snelling. He then purchased Denis Cherrier's claim in St. Paul. The cabin Campbell built on the corner of today's Kellogg Boulevard and St. Peter Street later became Harriet Bishop's school house.

Scott Campbell and Elizabeth Beaulieu's heritage was typical of the marriages that linked Native American women with men of European backgrounds. In those early years, Native Americans in considerable numbers gravitated about St. Paul, Mendota, Kaposia and Red Rock. They had furs, game and fish to sell or to trade for supplies. Most of these Native Americans were members of the Dakota river bands, but the Ojibway also frequented the area. The long-running enmity between the Dakota and the Ojibway occasionally erupted into open warfare. In 1842, the battle of Kaposia was fought by warriors from both sides. Incessant gunfire, which lasted for several hours, could be heard in St. Paul. Both sides sustained heavy losses until the Ojibway began to retreat, with the Dakota pursuing them toward Stillwater.

In 1853, more than ten years later, a fight broke out in downtown St. Paul at a trading post, operated by William H. Forbes, near today's Jackson Street and Kellogg Boulevard. A number of Ojibway attacked several Dakota who had come up the river from Kaposia to trade at Forbes' Minnesota Outfit. A Dakota woman was mortally wounded during a brief exchange of gunfire.

Joseph Renshaw Brown, legislator and editor.

In its early years, St. Paul's first residents bought, sold and traded their claims with bewildering rapidity. Henry Jackson, who was born in Virginia, arrived and bought from Benjamin Gervais a tract of land that today is located between Robert and Jackson streets. (Jackson Street is named for him.) With a small stock of goods, he opened a trading post and prospered. In 1846, he became St. Paul's first postmaster; the "post office," set up in his store, was a rude wooden case about two feet square with pigeonholes.

Two years earlier, Louis Robert, who had been born in Carondelet, Missouri, arrived from Prairie du Chien and bought property for $300 that thirty years later was worth several million dollars — part of Gervais' claim and all of Pig's Eye Parrant's claim at the Lower Landing. Robert had been a fur trader on the upper Missouri. As one of the original proprietors of the town when it finally was surveyed and laid out in 1847, he played a major role in establishing St. Paul as capital of the Territory of Minnesota. His warehouse at the foot of Jackson Street was the first frame house in St. Paul, built for him by Charles Bazille, a French Canadian carpenter who also built the first grist and saw mill on Phalen Creek. Robert Street is named for Louis Robert.

Joseph R. Brown was a fur trader, lumberman, land speculator, legislator and newspaper editor. Born in Maryland in 1805, he joined the army and arrived at Mendota in 1819 to help build Fort Snelling. While stationed at the fort, he was the Old Fort Snelling Dramatic Club's first "leading lady." Exploring the surrounding countryside, he traced Minnehaha Creek to its source in Lake Minnetonka. Minnehaha Falls originally was known as Brown's Falls. Brown became editor of the MINNESOTA PIONEER after James M. Goodhue's death.

Norman Wolford Kittson, early St. Paul entrepreneur.

As the PIONEER's editor, he took part in one of the great journalistic battles of the 1850s. This was the appointment as territorial printer, a political plum that often made the difference between solvency and bankruptcy for a frontier publisher. Brown made ingenious use of his appointment in 1853 and 1854. He sat up all one night writing a "Bill to Suppress Immorality," inveighing, among other things, against housewives who hung "undergarments" out to dry in Rice Park. Then he introduced his bill into the Territorial Senate, where he conveniently served as a senator. There he moved that the bill be read by title and printed. The motion carried and Brown pocketed payment for the printing costs.

Allied to the Dakota bands through his marriage to the daughter of a Dakota chief, Brown later served as an agent for the Dakota. He also laid out the town of Henderson; Brown's Valley and Brown County are named for him.

The role of Norman W. Kittson as one of the most significant of Minnesota's pioneers has been largely overshadowed by his friends and business partners, James J. Hill and Henry H. Sibley. Born in Canada in 1814, Kittson was the grandson of an officer who had served under Wolfe at Quebec. After his grandfather's death, Kittson's grandmother married Alexander Henry, the great explorer. Kittson became Sibley's partner in the American Fur Company. Together they built a string of posts in the region around Pembina, now in North Dakota, where Kittson had his

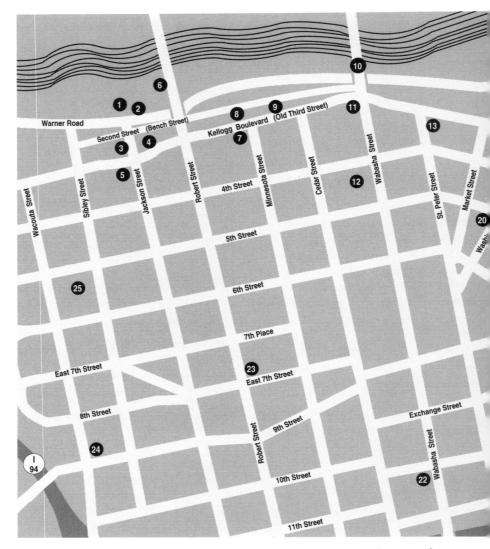

headquarters. He moved to St. Paul in 1855 and nine years later, with James J. Hill, formed the Red River Transportation Company. Originally the company operated steamboats on the Red River. Eventually the two men, with their Canadian partners and financiers, acquired the St. Paul and Pacific Railroad and built it into the Great Northern.

Kittson amassed a fortune through these ventures and in real estate. Kittson's addition stretched from the Mississippi to Twelfth Street and Lowertown to Market Street, the heart of today's downtown. He built the Globe office building and a mansion on the site of the present St. Paul Cathedral. His pride and joy was Kittsondale, a million-dollar stable and racetrack, at what is today Snelling and University avenues. He also owned Erdheim, a world-famous horse farm outside of Philadelphia, where Iroquoise, the first American horse to win the British Derby, was raised and trained.

Kittson is known to have had at least two and perhaps four Native American wives before marrying Mary A. Kittson of Fort Garry. His will

Some pioneer St. Paul sites, located on a modern street map:

1. Lower Landing
2. Louis Robert's warehouse and home
3. Henry Jackson's cabin
4. W. H. Forbe's Minnesota Outfit
5. St. Paul House
6. Pierre "Pig's Eye" Parrant's tavern
7. Central House
8. Small graveyard
9. Chapel of St. Paul, on Bench Street between Kellogg Boulevard and Warner Road
10. St. Paul Bridge
11. Vetal Guerin's cabin
12. Ramsey County Courthouse
13. Scott Campbell's cabin/Harriet Bishop's schoolhouse
14. Edward Phelan's cabin
15. Upper Landing
16. Irvine Park
17. American House
18. John Irvine's house
19. Rice Park
20. St. Paul City Hall
21. Assumption Church and school
22. First Territorial and State Capitol
23. St. James African Episcopal Church
24. First Baptist Church
25. Smith/Mears Park

mentioned eleven children, five of whom were Mary's; but based on a genealogical chart drawn up by his grandson, he apparently had twenty-six children. According to family tradition, Kittson acknowledged and provided for all of them.

While Kittson County is named for him, Kittson is perhaps best remembered for his Red River ox carts. These were two-wheeled, oxen-drawn wooden carts widely used by Native Americans for buffalo hunts. Kittson adapted them to haul furs from Pembina to St. Paul. With their wooden axles devoid of grease, their "big squeal" could be heard for miles. Their drivers, called *bois brules*, represented a mingling of French, Scotch, English, Cree and Ojibway; they wore coarse blue cloth with a profusion of brass buttons and a red sash about their waists.

The first train with six carts arrived in St. Paul in 1844, carrying $1,400 in furs. Their commerce left approximately $12,000, spent for supplies, in the tills of St. Paul traders. Within twenty years, more than $250,000 in raw pelts, buffalo robes, foodstuffs and pemmican (dried

With their wooden wheels and "big squeal," the famed Red River ox carts hauled supplies to Pembina and furs, pemmican and other goods to St. Paul.

meat mixed with tallow) were being hauled into St. Paul on the Red River carts. Buffalo robes and pemmican, in particular, often proceeded to eastern ports where they were shipped out to British troops fighting in the Crimea. Thus, St. Paul was a world trade center before it was a capital of a territory or of a state. Brown, Jackson and Kittson represented another growing group in pioneer St. Paul: the "old-stock North Americans" whose ancestors had lived in the eastern United States or Canada for several generations. They were joined by others of like background and ability, including Henry H. Sibley, John R. Irvine, Henry M. Rice, and Alexander Ramsey, in directing the affairs of the developing community for the next forty years.

The triangle of land between the Mississippi and the St. Croix rivers had been part of St. Croix County, Territory of Wisconsin, since 1840, with Stillwater as the county seat. When Wisconsin was admitted to the union in 1848, its western boundary was established at the St. Croix River. The land west of the river suddenly became a region without law or government, although it was referred to as the "rump" Territory of Wisconsin.

Alarmed, a group of St. Paul men met at Henry Jackson's store. (It couldn't have been a large group, J. Fletcher Williams wrote later, "for there were scarcely twenty English-speaking men in St. Paul... .") Actually, they probably met in the street; as one old settler pointed out, most such meetings were held in the street because there was more room and there were plenty of logs for seats. The meeting resulted in a convention, held August 26 in Stillwater. There, Henry H. Sibley was elected delegate to Congress from Wisconsin Territory. His assignment: secure the organization of Minnesota Territory.

On March 3, 1849, a bill prepared by Senator Stephen A. Douglas of Illinois, proposing Minnesota as a territory, was approved, and the territory was established, with St. Paul as its capital. It took over a month for the news to reach St. Paul. The winter had been long and hard — the worst in many years. The anxious watchers in the little settlement were cut off by snow and ice from the outside world, except for the occasional mail carried overland from Prairie du Chien. On April 9, 1849, with the river opened to navigation, the steamboat, DR. FRANKLIN NO. 2, rounded the bend a mile below St. Paul in the midst of a violent wind and rain storm to bring the good news to St. Paul's settlers. The rejoicing was riotous.

Minnesota Territory was still little more than forest and prairie. St. Paul's population was listed as 910 in the territorial census (J. Fletcher Williams lists it as 840). James M. Goodhue declared that when he arrived that spring, there were only thirty buildings in the settlement. Although the town site of "Saint Paul Proper" had been surveyed in 1847, it wasn't until 1849 that the ninety-acre plat was entered and the lots or blocks deeded to each owner.

The effect of territorial status on St. Paul was immediate and profound. Within three weeks, the village doubled in size, and seventy new buildings were erected, bringing the total to 149 buildings. St. Paul's arcadian period, with its isolation and primitive simplicity, was over.

The organization of the territory soon was under way. Alexander Ramsey, a Pennsylvanian appointed territorial governor by President Zachary Taylor, arrived in May. Other territorial officers also drifted in: Aaron Goodrich from Tennessee, chief justice; Charles Kilgore Smith from Ohio, secretary of state; Colonel Alexander M. Mitchell (another Ohioan),

Minnesota's first capitol (top of the photo, with the dome) was one of the more impressive sights in downtown St. Paul in 1856. It was destroyed by fire in 1881, and a second capitol built on the same site.

marshal; and Henry L. Moss from New York, district attorney. Seated on beds or trunks in a small room at the Saint Paul House on Third Street, and using a washstand as a desk, the men drew up the "First of June Proclamation" announcing the territorial government organized. St. Paul was incorporated as a town (it would be incorporated as a city in 1854); Ramsey County, its northern boundary extending to Lake Mille Lacs, was one of nine counties carved out of the surrounding wilderness, with St. Paul as its county seat. The territorial legislature began its deliberations in the first "capitol," the Central House, a two-story frame building on Bench Street near Minnesota.

Almost immediately, the legislature plunged into a spirited controversy over the capital's permanent location. It was the first of several debates that would arise in the next few years. This one ended in a draw. Undeterred,the legislators drafted plans for the building that was erected in 1851 as the first of two capitols on the same site at Tenth and Wabasha streets. The first Ramsey County Courthouse was built on "courthouse square," the block bounded by Cedar and Wabasha, Fourth and Fifth streets. The city hall was built in 1857 on the site of Landmark Center.

Harriet Bishop, educator and humanitarian.

In the meantime, the first schools had been established. Harriet Bishop arrived from Vermont in 1847. She was lured west by a missionary spirit and a despairing letter from Dr. Thomas Williamson, missionary at Kaposia, describing the "deplorable educational and religious condition" of the people of St. Paul. Like others laboring on the frontier, Williamson had another concern. Alcoholism continued to be a grave problem among the settlers, the native bands and the army at Fort Snelling. Temperance movements were growing in the eastern United States and Williamson wanted to strengthen the movement. The Temperance House, also known at Moffett's Castle, was established by Lott Moffett as a hotel that did not sell liquor. Harriet Bishop, a devout Baptist, helped organize St. Paul's first temperance society.

Harriet Bishop was a remarkable young woman who described herself, with a typically Victorian flourish, as a "feeble and timid young lady." She apparently was neither. An early newspaper editor described her as "angular, positive, determined — such a woman as is necessary for frontier life...tall, with a good figure; a bright, expressive face; earnest and decided in manners, and quick in speech." Her first view of St. Paul, from a canoe paddled by two young Dakota women, was dismaying.

"A cheerless prospect" greeted her, she wrote later. "A few log huts composed the town, three families the American population. With one of these [J. R. Irvine]...a home was offered me. Theirs was...the only [dwelling] of respectable size, containing three rooms and an attic."

Harriet Bishop organized a Sunday School and taught a day school for a year. Attendance was small — nine or ten at first — and an interpreter was needed for those who spoke only French or Dakota. Her schoolhouse was the cabin Scott Campbell had built at Third and St. Peter. The school soon expanded into larger quarters. After St. Paul's incorporation in 1849, the town was divided into three school districts, and Harriet Bishop continued to teach in one of them.

Several other schools important to St. Paul's early history were founded in the next few years: the Baldwin School established by the Reverend Edward Duffield Neill on the present site of Landmark Center; Assumption School, the oldest building still standing in downtown St. Paul, at 68 Exchange Street; and St. Joseph's Academy, also still standing at 355 Marshall Avenue but with origins tracing back to the little Chapel of St. Paul where the Sisters of St. Joseph first established a school in its vestry. (The Sisters also founded St. Joseph's Hospital, the first hospital in Minnesota, to care for the sick in the wake of the cholera epidemic of 1853.)

Angelina Jackson, one of St. Paul's first settlers.

Harriet Bishop is widely regarded as St. Paul's first school teacher and Harriet Island is named for her. She was preceded, if briefly, by Matilda Rumsey, who established a small school in a log building near the Upper Landing and taught there for a few months. Both Matilda Rumsey and Harriet Bishop were among several extraordinary women who endured the hardships of St. Paul's early years.

Others included Mary Turpin, who married Captain Louis Robert in St. Louis when she was thirteen years old. She arrived in St. Paul with her husband in 1844 when the only other white women in the settlement were Mary Ann Perry, Angelina Jackson, Genevieve Gervais and Rose Clewett. Mary Robert often accompanied her husband on fur-trading expeditions, camping out in a tent or cabin. She and Louis Robert had several children, but only two daughters lived to adulthood.

Mrs. Jeremiah Selby arrived in St. Paul with her husband in 1849. The farm they opened along today's Selby and Summit avenues became the site first of Norman W. Kittson's imposing mansion and later the

James M. Goodhue,
MINNESOTA PIONEER *editor.*

present Cathedral of St. Paul. Mrs. M. L. Stokes established the town's first millinery store on the corner of Third and Washington, where she also ran a boarding house. Angelina Bivens married Henry Jackson in Buffalo, New York, in 1838 and accompanied him to Minnesota four years later. Widowed only a few years after their arrival in St. Paul, both Mrs. Jackson and Mrs. Selby soon remarried and moved away.

The number of steamboats docking at the levee was rising steadily, from forty-one in 1844 to ninety-five in 1848. The first newspaper in Minnesota, the MINNESOTA PIONEER, was launched by James M. Goodhue in 1849. The following year, Goodhue issued the town's first business directory. It listed five clergymen, fourteen lawyers, two land agents, four doctors, sixteen mercantile firms, one shoemaker, six hotels, three painters, two black-smiths, four plasterers, five masons, eighteen carpenters, one silversmith, one gunsmith, five bakers, three wheelwrights, one harness maker and one tinner.

The 1850 census listed 1,294 residents of St. Paul and 257 families. About ninety residents listed Canada as their birthplace; more than sixty claimed Ireland as their homeland, while England and Germany were each declared the birthplaces of about twenty residents. Most of St. Paul's settlers were from the East Coast or New England, but "Isabelle Edes" was born in Norway and "Mary Leolter," whose husband, Charles, was from Ireland, was a native of Spain.

Unquestionably, the rush to settlement was on. It was spurred by an event that had tragic consequences for those most directly involved: the Mdewakanton bands of the Dakota people living along the Mississippi and Minnesota rivers across from St. Paul, and the Wahpekute, Sisseton and Wahpeton bands in southern and western Minnesota. With the treaties of Traverse des Sioux and Mendota in 1851, the Dakota were forced to give up most of their land, leaving them with just two narrow reservations, the Upper and Lower reservations which stretched along the upper Minnesota River in the western part of the state. The move to the reservations in 1853 and 1854 was only marginally successful. Paid less than the land was worth and promised benefits that too often failed to materialize, the Dakota soon became disillusioned. Promises were broken on both sides and some of the Dakota, including members of the Mdewakanton bands, began to drift back to their old homes near St. Paul. Tensions grew, particularly among the Dakota who had remained in western Minnesota, and in August, 1862, they erupted into the warfare that has become known as the Dakota Conflict.

In the meantime, newcomers crowding into St. Paul were creating a culturally diverse community. Jacob W. Bass, who established the Saint Paul House at Third and Jackson streets, has been described as the first German to arrive in St. Paul. Bass, however, was born in Vermont. One of the first immigrants from Germany was Bartlett Presley, a successful trader who was born in Baden. Theodore Hamm, also from Baden, and Gustav Willius and Henry Meyer from Bremen, arrived in 1856. Hamm owned a boarding house before going into the brewery business; and Willius and Meyer founded a business venture that grew into the German-American Bank. (Years later, the bank merged with the First National Bank of St. Paul.)

By 1860, Ramsey County had become one of Minnesota's largest German enclaves. This was due partly to the great wave of emigration from Germany to the United States following the Revolution of 1848 — one of the most famous of nineteenth century Europe's political upheavals. St. Paul had a German Emigration Society as early as 1858. The Germans settled first in the Fifth Ward around the first German Catholic Church, Assumption Church, organized in 1855 on Exchange Street. The parish supported a benevolent society and operated a boarding house for homeless workers. Germans also settled in the Eighth Ward, around St. Agnes Church (where confessions were heard in German as recently as the 1960s).

According to the 1860 census, most of these German immigrants had Bavarian or Prussian backgrounds. They brought to their new homes a love of music and theater; such societies as the Turnverein; German language newspapers (the DAILY VOLKS ZEITUNG appeared in 1855); and, above all, that major contribution to the state's economy, the breweries.

What is now the West Side, pictured here in 1869, was part of the Township of West St. Paul in the 1850s and 1860s. Many of the community's settlers were German, Irish, French Canadian and Danish.

In 1848, Anthony Yoerg established the first brewery in Minnesota near Eagle Street in Upper Town. Later, he moved it to the West Side*. In 1854, the German Reading Society was incorporated. Four years later, the German community built the Atheneum, a one-story frame structure at Walnut and Exchange streets that became a popular gathering place.

Among the first wave of immigrants from Germany to reach St. Paul were the early members of the Jewish community. Joseph Ullman, who was in the liquor business, had emigrated from French Alsace. His wife, Amelia, was another sorely tried but persevering pioneer wife. This poignant account of life in a town whose hotels and boarding houses were so crowded that people camped in the streets is in the Minnesota Historical Society collections:

> *"Only a conscientious housewife, only a devoted mother who had lived in St. Paul in those days knows all the inconveniences and miseries that I was forced to endure.... Every drop of water used had to be carried across the prairie from a well in a livery stable.... My child was ill much of the time from lack of proper nourishment, for good wholesome food was difficult to obtain. Fresh vegetables and fruit were unknown. These things being brought up from St. Louis by the boats, they were often in such a condition upon their arrival at St. Paul that their use would have been deleterious to health."*

Amelia Ullman, pioneer housewife and an early member of Mount Zion Temple.

Joseph and Amelia Ullman became part of a small group of Jewish men and women who organized Mount Zion Hebrew Congregation in 1856. Among the other founders were Henry Cali (or Cole), Jacob Newman, Morris and Henry Marks, and Benjamin, Isidor and Emanuel Rose. The Rose brothers had arrived in St. Paul directly from Bavaria. Most of the synagogue's founders were in the clothing or liquor business, but Ullman, forsaking liquor for furs, built up a world-wide business with branches in New York, London and Leipzig.

Despite the fact that they were outnumbered by the German population, it was the Irish immigrants who left an indelible stamp on St. Paul. A partial explanation might lie in their domination of St. Paul politics, and their fraternity

---

*While the Mississippi River flows from north to south, it curves toward the northeast as it enters St. Paul. Therefore, while the land across the river from downtown St. Paul lies on the river's west bank, it is south of downtown St. Paul.

in such organizations as the Benevolent Society of Erin and the Shields Guards — a militia named for General James Shields. Further explanation might lie in the sense of community displayed in their vigorous promotion of such cultural celebrations as their St. Patrick's Day parades, the first of which was held in 1851. The "impromptu celebration" included a flag-raising, speeches and a fired salute. A hastily-prepared supper at Barney Rogers was topped off by a 300-person parade, led by a band, up the village's principal streets. "The procession," the MINNESOTA PIONEER reported, "returned to the scene of the evening's festivities about nine o'clock where numerous gentlemen made addresses appropriate for the occasion. The company dispersed at an early hour, highly pleased with the first celebration of St. Patrick's Day in Minnesota. May there be many such."

Father John Ireland, later Archbishop Ireland, as he appeared in 1862.

While Irish immigrants settled on farms in communities such as Credit River in Scott County and Shieldsville near Faribault, many of them imitated their brethren in the East and gravitated toward the relative security of work in the cities. More than half of the Irish in St. Paul in 1850 were unskilled laborers.

By 1858, however, six of the city's eleven policemen were Irish; twenty years later, a third of the force was Irish. The spread of Irish immigrants throughout the city is indicated by the development of their churches. At first, most Irish attended the cathedral. Within ten years after the end of the Civil War, however, they had organized new parishes on both the West Side and the East Side.

A characteristic of Irish Catholic life that paralleled Protestant life at that time was the presence of a strong temperance movement. It was a thread running through American social history, as groups throughout the country were attempting to come to grips with the problem of alcohol consumption as they also tried to cope with change. Bishop Cretin organized the Catholic Temperance Society of St. Paul in 1852; the cause was taken up later by Archbishop John Ireland, one of the best known and most illustrious of the Irish of St. Paul. Rivaling the archbishop as a prominent leader with Irish ancestry was his friend and associate, James J. Hill, the "empire builder" who founded the Great Northern Railroad. Hill had arrived in 1856 as a young man from a farm near Toronto, to take a job as a clerk with the Dubuque and St. Paul Packet Company.

As early as 1852, Swedish immigrants began to settle in St. Paul. The appropriately named First Lutheran Church was founded two years later.

It was the first Lutheran church in Minnesota, and like other early churches, its beginning was rocky. Members met in homes. Not until 1867 did the congregation raise enough money to erect a building on the west side of the Phalen Creek valley.

The middle 1850s were characterized by wild speculation in real estate as settlers flooded into the territory. In 1854, speculator Henry McKenty bought several thousand acres of prairie for $1.25 an acre and sold it the next year for $5 an acre. In 1855, 30,000 people were reported to have landed in St. Paul. In 1857, the city's population stood at close to 10,000. Minnesota's first real estate boom was on, and the cost of money was enormous — 42 percent interest a year for working capital.

In 1857, the bubble burst. The bankruptcy of a New York financial institution, the Ohio Life Insurance and Trust Company, set off a serious economic debacle that was national in scope. In Minnesota, cash dried up, real estate speculators and merchants were ruined, banks closed, people were thrown out of work, St. Paul lost half of its population, and Ramsey County was forced to issue scrip.

Trauma of another kind had been inflicted on St. Paul earlier that year. A bill to move the capital from St. Paul to St. Peter had, to the dismay of the city's residents, passed the legislature. It was on its way to enrollment and signature by the governor when Joe Rolette, chairman of the Enrollment Committee, intervened.

The story is one of the best-known in Minnesota's history. Rolette was a popular and intelligent French Canadian. The son of an important fur trader in Prairie du Chien, Rolette was at this juncture the legislative representative from Pembina. He was a colorful man who wore Indian garb at home, possessed a well-known sense of humor, and — most importantly — was sympathetic to St. Paul's cause.

Rolette simply tucked the bill into his pocket, walked over to Truman and Smith's bank, locked it in the vault and hid out at the Fuller House in Lowertown. Reportedly, he whiled away the time playing cards while friends gravely reported him heading north on his dog sled. When the time for the bill to become law had expired, Rolette reappeared with it. Subsequent legal opinion held that the bill had not passed and St. Paul remained the capital.

During the winter of 1857, a constitutional convention met in St. Paul to prepare Minnesota for statehood. The convention split immediately along party lines, with the Republicans and Democrats meeting separately and drafting two separate constitutions. Since their rancorous differences not only courted national ridicule but legal challenges as well, cooler heads

Legislator Joe Rolette, who is credited with blocking an attempt to make St. Peter the state capital.

prevailed and the two constitutions were combined. On August 28, 1857, both conventions adopted the constitution. It was ratified on October 13, 1857, and on May 11, 1858, Minnesota was admitted to the Union as the thirty-second state.

The 1857 census, compiled in preparation for statehood, lists St. Paul's population at 9,973: 1,700 residents were natives of the

The Fuller House in Lowertown, as it appeared when the wily Joe Rolette hid out there, was one of St. Paul's early hotels. Later the International Hotel, the building was destroyed by fire in 1869.

United States; the remainder represented more than twenty other countries. Again, the largest group of immigrants were the Germans, who numbered 1,350. Irish-born immigrants made up the second largest group. Italy was listed as the birthplace of a twenty-year-old woman, M. Bonfante, and Cuba the birthplace of a soldier discharged from Fort Snelling whose wife was from Ireland. The jobs these residents held were diverse and many obsolete occupations were noted; but the real estate mania was apparent in listings like "land buyer" and "land agent." In 1859, 30 percent of the state's population was foreign-born. Immigration records indicate that while the heads of families might have been born abroad, the subsequent birthplaces of their children sometimes reveal the family's migration across the United States.

Henry Hastings Sibley, the state's first governor.

When the word reached St. Paul on May 14, 1858, that Minnesota had been admitted to the Union, there were no celebrations. Henry Hastings Sibley was quietly sworn as the state's first governor. J. M. Cavanaugh and W. W. Phelps prepared to leave for Washington as representatives, and Henry M. Rice and General James Shields as senators. Within a year, with the first export of grain from Minnesota, prosperity again seemed to be in the air. But in these years just before the Civil War, there was also a sense of foreboding. As J. Fletcher Williams wrote: "The disunion cloud was darkening the southern horizon and the mutterings of war were heard in the distance." Had the governments in St. Paul and Washington been listening closely, they also would have heard the mutterings in the lodges of the desperately unhappy and disillusioned Dakota bands on their reservations.

In 1860, Republican Alexander Ramsey was elected governor after a bitter political campaign against Democrat George Becker. At a time when aliens could vote four months after applying for citizenship, both candidates were well aware of the voting power of the foreign-born and set out to exploit it. The Republican platform proscribed "no man on account of his religion or nativity," called for free land for settlers, and declared that the party was opposed to any "discrimination between native and naturalized citizens" as well as to any attempt to curtail naturalization rights. Not to be outdone, the Democrats adopted similar platform language. The Republicans swept the election, however, taking not only the governorship but also two congressional seats and many legislative chairs.

In April, 1861, Ramsey was in Washington. He remembered the day the Civil War began:

"The knots of earnest men...in the corridors and reading rooms of the hotels indicated...that there was an impending peril. On Saturday night, April 13th, the population of Washington was deeply moved by the intelligence that Fort Sumter...had been attacked...and that the garrison had surrendered. Early Sunday morning...I visited the war department and found Secretary [of War Simon P.] Cameron...about to leave his office.

"I said, 'My business is simply as governor of Minnesota to tender a thousand men to defend the government.'

" 'Sit down immediately,' he replied, 'and write the tender you have made, as I am now on my way to the President's mansion.'

"This was quickly done and thus Minnesota became the first to cheer President Lincoln by offers of assistance in the crisis which had arrived."

Ramsey was notified that Minnesota's quota of the 75,000 men Lincoln called for would be one regiment of 780 men. The regiment was assembled from groups of militia that had been formed in the 1850s, among them the Pioneer Guard and the St. Paul Volunteers. Organized in 1856, the Pioneer Guard was the state's first volunteer military organization. It was much in demand for balls and parades. Its members drilled faithfully at Armory Hall, the third floor of the Bernheimer Block — part of which still exists within the former YWCA building on Kellogg Boulevard. The Guard was organized into Company A of the First

Alexander Ramsey, governor at the start of the Civil War.

The First Minnesota Battalion, Volunteer Infantry, shown here at Fort Snelling in 1863, was a successor to the original First Minnesota.

Minnesota Infantry Regiment by its commander, Alexander Wilkin, who was secretary of the territory and had been a captain in the Mexican War. An orderly sergeant in the Guard, Josias King, is credited with being the first to step forward and sign the muster roll as a volunteer for Civil War service. A monument erected in 1903 in his honor still stands near the intersection of Summit and Marshall Avenues, below the St. Paul Cathedral.

While Wilkin organized Company A, William H. Acker resigned as adjutant general of Minnesota and organized the St. Paul Volunteers into Company C. Among the Volunteers was Marshall Sherman, who was St. Paul's first Congressional Medal of Honor winner and St. Paul's only medal winner of the Civil War years. He was decorated for bravery in seizing the battle flag of the Twenty-eighth Virginia Infantry Regiment during Pickett's charge on the final day of the battle of Gettysburg. After the war, Sherman established the Sherman House, a hotel at Fourth and Sibley streets. It was known as "the best two-dollar a day house in the country." Wilkin, while a colonel in command of a brigade, lost his life at the battle of Tupelo. He was Minnesota's highest ranking officer to be killed during the war.

Seven more military companies were organized in the spring of 1861 to complete the First Minnesota's roster. Most of its officers were St. Paul men: Willis A. Gorman (a former territorial governor), colonel; Dr. J. H. Stewart, surgeon; and the Reverend E. D. Neill, chaplain. Toward the end of the war, Neill became one of President Lincoln's secretaries.

Uniforms for the men were nonexistent. The new adjutant general, John B. Sanborn, placed an order with Culver and Farrington, a St. Paul dry goods and clothing store, for $10,488 worth of uniforms. The First Minnesota wore these picturesque uniforms through the first battle of Bull Run: red flannel shirts, black pantaloons and black felt slouch hats.

On June 22, 1861, the troops left Fort Snelling aboard two steamships, the WAR EAGLE and the NORTHERN BELLE. Put ashore at St. Paul's Upper Landing, they marched up the bluff, past the cheering crowds that lined

General John B. Sanborn, whose duties included ordering uniforms for the First Minnesota.

Third Street, to the Lower Landing. There they embarked again for the East.

Twenty-one units were recruited in Minnesota, including the Fifth Minnesota Infantry Regiment with Father John Ireland as its chaplain. Among the enlisted men were twenty-eight Murphys, twenty-five Kelleys, twenty-four Kellys, twenty-three Ryans, twenty O'Connors, as well as O'Sheas, Mahoneys, Maloneys, Callahans, Cassidys, Delanys, Daleys, Dohenys, Bruns, O'Neils, Tierneys, O'Briens, O'Gradys, Collins, Buckleys, Hanleys, McCartys, McCoys, Noonans, Finnegans, Flanagans, Quinns, Kilpatricks and Kirkpatricks.

The First Minnesota became the most famous of Minnesota's Civil War regiments because of its courageous charge of Confederate lines during the second day of the battle of Gettysburg. Only forty-seven of the 262 men available for action survived the charge. In tribute, the number was used many years later to designate the Forty-seventh Division of Minnesota's National Guard.

Even as the First Minnesota was being mustered, St. Paul was plunging enthusiastically into the war effort. Spirits were high. The April 17, 1861, St. Paul Press reported that the city was laden with patriotic decorations: "The ladies were all out shopping, amid all the wind and dust, but all they inquired for was for bunting."

Thirty-nine firemen responded to the call for volunteers, and so many policemen that Mayor John Prince told the City Council that it was "impossible for the present number of men to thoroughly guard the city." He called for the entire police force, except for the chief and a captain, to be dismissed so they could enter the army and asked the citizens to form a volunteer night patrol or home guard.

The City Council itself lost two members to the war effort when Aldermen D. H. Valentine and H. P. Grant enlisted. Their colleagues on the Council agreed to hold their seats open and to appropriate $120 of city funds for each man to buy the sword, belt and sash that were "appropriate to his rank."

St. Paul's generosity in providing funds for soldiers' families was almost its undoing. The Council had voted to provide each family with $5 per month. By 1863, however, the Council had to cut costs by compensating only those families with children, and then at a rate of just $1 a month for each woman and child.

The women of St. Paul organized the St. Paul Volunteer Aid Society, believed to be the first of its kind in the country. They scraped lint, rolled bandages, baked pies and made almost 900 emergency cases and twenty-five oilcloth guard cases. They supplied the troops with needle books, mosquito face nets, and 600 havelocks, a linen attachment for a cap that protected the neck from the sun.

They sewed all this in stifling heat, that first summer of the war, as they gathered in Ingersoll Hall, a two-story building on the southeast corner of Bridge Square, the intersection today of Kellogg Boulevard and Wabasha Street. "Ladies having sewing machines are called upon to lend a hand," the ST. PAUL PIONEER AND DEMOCRAT urged.

Amelia Ullman remembered wartime St. Paul — perhaps before the reality of the casualty lists set in:

"Recruiting stations were established at St. Paul. Patriotism became intense. Everywhere was there the sound of the fife and drum, the splendor of new uniforms and the burnishing of new arms. Homes were broken up by the departure of fathers and sons; the boat landing was almost daily the scene of sad partings."

Early in 1865, a "sanitary fair" was held in St. Paul by the Minnesota branch of the United States Sanitary Commission. Raffles, food sales, and a grand ball raised $13,496 for the benefit of soldiers in military hospitals. One historian noted that women stepped into men's jobs in the face of some labor shortages. This was another instance in American history of women taking over the jobs of men who had volunteered for army service. At least two Minnesota women apparently enlisted in the army and fought beside the men. An article published in a St. Paul newspaper in 1912 gave the following account:

"A Mrs. Clayton who, when very young, was in 1856 married in [St. Paul]...insisted on accompanying her husband when he announced his intention to enlist. Finding it impossible to dissuade her, Clayton procured for her a suit of man's clothes and a false mustache, and the couple were mustered into Co. A, 13th Missouri cavalry, they being in St. Louis at the outbreak of the war."

"She was," the newspaper continued, "a bold rider, a brave soldier and afraid of nothing." She served for almost two years. She was wounded twice during the battle of Shiloh and again at the battle of Murfreesboro where her husband was killed. His death ended her career as a soldier. She was discharged after telling her commanding officer who she was.

Another newspaper story told of a boyish-looking orderly who appeared at Fort Snelling as a member of a squad of men who were joining a regiment of mounted rangers. The headquarters officer was at first puzzled but concluded that the young man was simply under age. At about the same time, the newspaper account continued, the young daughter of a well-to-do Minnesota family had disappeared without a trace. Her father found her at the fort, masquerading as the orderly.

The incidence of women posing as men in order to join the army was not high during the Civil War, but it also was not unusual, military historians maintain. Mrs. Clayton herself reported that she had seen other women in the Union ranks.

As the war ground on, patriotism began to wear thin and a controversial draft was set in motion. St. Paul newspapers reported a confrontation between enrolling officers and provost marshalls, and women and children in a Lowertown neighborhood between Jackson Street, Dayton's Bluff, Sixth Street and the river. The women refused to reveal the names of men eligible for conscription, and a fight began. Attempts to arrest the most belligerent of the women met with a vehement response as one woman picked up an ax and another scuffled with an officer. In other instances, women locked their doors to keep draft workers from entering, threw dirty water on the workers and threatened them with shovels. There also were men who tried to dodge service. One, according to a news account, pleaded insanity as an excuse for not serving. Ordered to enlist anyway, he jumped out a third-story window overlooking Eagle Street. Although badly hurt, he nevertheless was sent south when he recovered.

Minnesota Civil War veterans regrouped in 1905, for a parade from the old capitol to the new one. The parade marked the transfer of battle flags.

Fourteen months after the first troops left Minnesota, and while the men who governed the state from St. Paul were preoccupied with the pressing demands of the Union forces, a tragic conflict erupted little more than 100 miles to the west. The bitterness and discouragement of the Dakota bands confined to their strips of reservation along the upper Minnesota River broke into the open with the Dakota Conflict of 1862.

The Dakota had been cheated for years by unscrupulous traders. Their annuity payments were delayed by a government distracted by the Civil War; and they were at the mercy of Indian

Members of Dakota Mdewakanton and Wahpekute tribes visited Washington, D. C., in 1858 to negotiate a treaty.

agents who were political appointees and unqualified to work with the tribes. The Dakota living on the Upper and Lower Reservations grew increasingly angry and frustrated. By August of 1862, they were starving and penniless. When their annuity payments did not arrive, traders at the reservations refused to extend any more credit.

The Dakota Conflict which erupted was a last, desperate attempt to drive the settlers from southern Minnesota. The Dakota, however, were divided into a war and a peace party. A war party was led with reluctance by Little Crow, even as a peace party formed around Chief Wabasha. Hostilities broke out on August 18, and within two days the entire frontier was aflame. In St. Paul, Governor Ramsey pleaded with the government in Washington to halt recruitment for the Union army so he could assemble a force to protect the frontier.

"No one not there can conceive the panic in the state," he added. Many of the settlers abandoned their farms and fled into the nearest town or to Fort Ridgely. Others arrived in St. Paul. Some never returned to those farms. On August 26, Lincoln responded:

"Yours received. Attend to the Indians. If the draft cannot proceed of

Little Crow VI, who reluctantly led the Dakota Conflict of 1862.

course it will not proceed. Necessity knows no law. The Government cannot extend the time. A. Lincoln."

Within less than five weeks, the conflict ended with the battle of Wood Lake, a defeat that was a disaster for the Native Americans. Many of the Dakota warriors fled into the Dakotas; others surrendered to troops commanded by Henry H. Sibley. The captives were held that winter in a camp at Fort Snelling. There they endured great suffering. In December, thirty-eight of the Dakota men were hanged in Mankato. That winter Congress abrogated its treaties with the Dakota people, confiscated their reservations and tribal funds, and moved them to a new reservation on the Missouri River. Fewer than 200 Dakota remained in the region around St. Paul.

Little Crow's fate was a sad reflection of the enmities of that period. After the fighting ended, the chief escaped with some of his followers into the Dakotas. The following summer of 1863, he was back in Minnesota. On July 3, while he was picking berries with his sixteen-year-old son in a little glade near Hutchinson, he was shot and killed by a party of hunters.

For a time, Little Crow's remains were exhibited by the Minnesota Historical Society, then placed in a vault. The frontier was closing, Little Crow's biographer, Gary Clayton Anderson, wrote, Minnesota was entering a new era, and the chief's remains, treated as curiosities, "became an embarrassment." In 1971, they were returned to his descendants for burial in Flandrau, South Dakota.

Throughout the 1860s, African Americans began to migrate to St. Paul in increasing numbers. They were drawn by the labor shortage created by the recruitment of men for the Union forces. In May, 1863, the steamboat NORTHERNER approached St. Paul laden with "contraband" laborers headed for jobs at Fort Snelling. The steamboat also was towing a raft with 176 African American men, women and children on board. Calling themselves "pilgrims," they were fugitive slaves led by a preacher, Robert Hickman. The steamboat had come upon the raft drifting in the Mississippi near Jefferson, Missouri, and took it in tow. They were followed a week later by a larger group of 218 — including a hundred women and children who were under the protective custody of a chaplain and escorted by an Iowa regiment. Some settled into jobs at Fort Snelling, but others followed Hickman into St. Paul.

Robert Hickman became the co-founder and the first pastor of Pilgrim Baptist Church, which was formally organized in 1866. The congregation's first church structure was built in 1870 at Thirteenth and Cedar streets. By 1900, the African American community had established four other churches. St. Mark's Episcopal Church was organized in 1867 but disbanded a year or so later. In 1894, St. Philip's Episcopal Church was formed. St. James African Methodist Church purchased its permanent home in 1881, and St. Peter Claver Catholic Church, founded in 1889, erected a building at Aurora and Farrington in 1892.

More than half of the African Americans who arrived in St. Paul after the Civil War were young, unmarried men. At first, they settled around the Lower Landing, and they found low-paying jobs as porters or waiters in the city's major hotels, such as the Metropolitan at Third and Washington —

The Lower Landing and Union Depot (shown at left) served as the major arrival and departure point for nineteenth century St. Paul.

By the 1880s, growth of the railroad industry established St. Paul as the region's transportation hub. In Lowertown, the railyards' location next to the Mississippi linked two means of transportation.

the site today of the Minnesota Club. By 1880 a major employer of blacks had been established in St. Paul — the railroads.

A railroad was first chartered by the legislature in 1857 and received a congressional land grant as the Minnesota and Pacific Railroad. Despite financial problems created by the Panic of 1857, most of its roadbed between St. Paul and St. Anthony had been graded by 1860. On September 9, 1861, a harbinger of vast change tied up at the Lower Landing. On board the steamboat ALHAMBRA and on accompanying barges was the locomotive, "William Crooks," as well as railroad cars and iron tracks.

In 1862, the railroad's name was changed to the St. Paul and Pacific. That spring, track was laid between the two towns and the first run over the new iron road was made by a party consisting of St. Paul's mayor, John S. Prince, the city's aldermen, and a joyous crowd of approximately one hundred. Economic distractions, however, had accompanied the Civil War. It was not until the late 1860s that lines were laid to link St. Paul with St. Cloud, Wayzata, Willmar, Breckenridge and Melrose.

Along the lines traveled the new immigrants who were crowding into St. Paul and moving on out into the state. Agricultural products flowed back into the city for shipment elsewhere. Towns that needed supplies to sell to the settlers were springing up along the rails.

As St. Paul began to emerge as the transportation hub of the region, the city began to change. Railroad depots dotted the downtown until 1879, when the railroads joined together to build the St. Paul Union Depot on the site of the St. Paul and Pacific's little depot (a block south of Third Street at Sibley). Additional rail lines constructed within the county opened suburban areas, such as Merriam Park and St. Anthony Park.

The city, itself, no longer contained in the old downtown neighborhood, began to spread outward into its first inner ring neighborhoods. Jobs for the German, Swedish and Irish laborers who were arriving by steamboat and rail also moved outward from the city. The North End, Frogtown, the East Side, the West Side, and the West Seventh Street neighborhoods filled up with the families of men who needed to be close to jobs with the railroads.

In 1872, the first horsecar plodded along a two-mile track from Seven Corners to Lafayette and Westminster. By 1870, St. Paul's population was 12,976. By 1880, it was 41,473. In 1874, the Wabasha Street bridge replaced the St. Paul bridge, erected as a toll bridge in 1859. Gas lamps lighted the downtown streets. St. Paul's Volunteer Firefighters, who had protected the city since the formation of the Hook and Ladder Company in 1854, reluctantly disbanded in 1877 as the city moved to a paid force. A velocipede mania seized the city and cyclists raced around Armory Hall. In 1873, the city-county hospital that would become Ancker Hospital was established. St. Paul's pioneer days were over.

Gas lights cast a warming glow on East Third Street during the 1887 Winter Carnival.

PART III:

COMING OF AGE
1880 – 1920

As St. Paul grew, the downtown and West Side communities saw many changes. In this 1886 photo, a recognizable skyline has taken shape downtown. The Robert Street bridge is under construction in the right background.

The impact of the railroads on nineteenth century St. Paul was enormous. They made the city the transportation center of the Upper Midwest and the gateway to the Northwest. They played a pivotal role in the closing of the frontier. They drew thousands upon thousands of newcomers, who enriched the city with their cultures, customs, and diversity. By 1880 the rail lines had passed Minnesota's boundaries in all directions and by 1893 they had reached the Pacific.

The United States of the 1880s was the target of a massive movement of immigrants and refugees, chiefly from Europe. Behind this movement lay political unrest, persecution, economic depressions, the emotional tug of letters to families and friends back home and the lure of greater opportunity.

Behind the movement also lay the efforts of such colonizers as Archbishop John Ireland and John Sweetman, founder of the Irish-American Colonization Society. Just as powerful a force was the State Board of Immigration. In an aggressive effort to recruit workers to build the railroads, farmers to till the soil, and merchants and tradesmen to supply the farmers, the board published pamphlets in German, Swedish, Norwegian, Welsh, and other languages. According to historian Theodore C. Blegen, the board advertised the state's virtues in an effort to establish immigrant colonies. The board sent agents to American seaports and to

Europe to recruit immigrants; persuaded railroads to provide lower fares for immigrants; and influenced the building of hotels to give immigrants a place to stay.

The need for such arrangements became apparent in St. Paul as early as 1867, when the first boat of the season docked and many of its passengers had nowhere to go. The St. Paul Board of Trade opened a "House for Emigrants" in a warehouse near the foot of Chestnut Street. This was a temporary shelter, providing bunks filled with straw, and stoves and fuel for cooking. Later, immigrants were housed in the Railroad Immigration House at Broadway and Third Street and in the Union Depot.

The nation itself seemed to be on the move. In 1888, a peak year, some eight million travelers passed through St. Paul's old Union Depot. Close to 150 trains arrived and departed every day. While many travelers were simply passing through, others stayed to help settle the city's first-ring neighborhoods beyond the downtown district. Blegen noted that from 1870 to 1920, census figures show that two-thirds or more of Minnesota's residents were foreign-born or the children of foreign-born parents. In fifteen years, St. Paul's population tripled, reaching 140,292 by 1895.

It was a prosperous period, despite the 1893 depression. The influx of immigrants led to a great building boom that changed the face of the city. As it left behind its frontier years, St. Paul replaced its frame houses and stubby business blocks with the often monumental structures that characterized America's vision of itself during that expansionist era. A massive new St. Paul City Hall-Ramsey County Courthouse was built at Fourth and Wabasha streets. When the state capitol at Tenth and Cedar burned down, a more imposing building went up on the same site. A new post office and federal building replaced the old city hall across from Rice

(Left) The Ramsey County Court House and St. Paul City Hall were housed in this building, built in 1884 at Fourth and Wabasha. (Right) The ornate, twelve-story Pioneer Press building was erected in 1889.

Park. In 1885, the National German-American Bank was built at Fourth and Robert; and in 1889 the twelve-story Pioneer Building, St. Paul's first skyscraper, also went up at Fourth and Robert.

Many of the buildings from that period can still be seen throughout the city: in Lowertown where warehouses replaced homes that once made the district an elegant residential neighborhood; around Irvine Park, near Seven Corners, where Alexander Ramsey built his mansion in 1872; and on Summit Avenue, Crocus Hill and Dayton's Bluff.

St. Paul in the 1880s clearly was a city in the grip of massive change. Change was reflected in the outward spread of its residents. Change was reflected in the development of transportation systems and of communication systems — such as the telephone — that would link new residents. And, change was reflected in the rise of social agencies that would help newcomers adjust to their new home.

On the front line of this adjustment were the churches, which were everywhere in St. Paul. Their genesis lay in the arrival on the frontier of such leaders as Father Augustin Ravoux, who succeeded Father Galtier as shepherd of the Catholic flock, and of the Reverend Edward Duffield Neill, who founded First Presbyterian Church, House of Hope Presbyterian Church, the Baldwin School and Macalester College.

From its beginning, St. Paul has maintained a predominantly Catholic stamp, although by 1880 the city's forty-nine congregations reflected a diversity of faiths as well as of cultures and settlement patterns. While the German Catholics settled around Assumption and St. Agnes churches, the French went to the Church of St. Louis at Tenth and Cedar, where French was spoken. The Irish were drawn to St. Mary's in Lowertown, St. Michael's on the West Side and St. John's on the East Side; Czechs and Poles worshipped at St. Stanislaus off West Seventh Street.

Pilgrim Baptist Church, the Church of St. Peter Claver, and St. James African Methodist Episcopal Church continued to serve the African American community that by the end of the nineteenth century was

Assumption School children lined up for a group picture in 1885. The church and school were a nucleus for the German Catholic community.

flowering in the neighborhood surrounding the now-vanished Rondo Street. Black masonry also was established in 1866 with the founding of the Pioneer Lodge of the Ancient Free and Accepted Masons.

Within the Jewish community, six synagogues had been established between 1872 and 1900 by distinct national groups. The Russian Jews were the driving force behind the Sons of Zion, organized in 1883. They congregated at Rutchik's Hay and Feed Store on the West Side, before building their new B'nai Zion synagogue in 1902. When B'nai Zion opened at 150 State Street, the crowd was so large that it broke the steps.

The Polish Jews contributed to the growth of Sons of Jacob, which moved to a new building in 1888. The Hebrew Ladies Benevolent Society was founded in 1871 as an organization of Mount Zion Temple. That same year, B'nai Brith was established in St. Paul. By 1900, Beth Hamedrash Hagodol, Sharey Hesed Woemet, and Sons of Abraham had formed.

Among the Protestants, First Baptist Church in Lowertown was such an early arrival in St. Paul that it gave its name to Baptist Hill, a fragment of which still exists as Mears Park. Market Street Methodist Church, on the site of today's Saint Paul Hotel, had a more ecumenical past. When the Methodists who built it moved on, the church sheltered a Swedenborgian congregation. Later, Archbishop Ireland acquired the church for Italian and African American Catholics. By 1904, the building had become an automobile garage.

The Italians moved from the Market Street Methodist Church to the basement of the cathedral. By 1914, two church buildings were housing Italian Catholics: Holy Redeemer on College Avenue and St. Ambrose on

Mount Zion Temple, founded in 1856, was St. Paul's first synagogue. Shown here as it appeared in 1875 at Tenth and Minnesota, Mount Zion moved to Avon and Holly after the turn-of-the-century.

Children in red, white and blue capes and caps form a "living flag" in front of Central Presbyterian Church. (Note the stars atop some caps.) The picture dates from 1903-1905.

the East Side. In the meantime, Father Nicholas Odone had arrived in 1899 to take charge of the Italian mission. He introduced St. Paul's Columbus Day celebrations in 1904, and he founded the Mount Carmel Societies for Women and the St. Antonio de Padua Benefit Society. He also was active in fostering the two Italian congregations.

Neill's House of Hope Presbyterian Church and the Episcopalians' Christ Church, whose slender "holy toothpick" steeple pierced the sky over Third Street, drew the city's Yankees. Lutheran congregations appeared with the influx of Swedish, Norwegian, Danish and German Lutherans. Minneapolis has long had the image of a Scandinavian city, but the Swedes were the third largest ethnic group in St. Paul, after the Germans and the Irish.

For some newcomers, such as the Irish, their churches were primarily places of worship. For others, churches were social service centers. The words of an Italian descendant reflect this: "We went there for mass. If we wanted to have a social, we had it at the church. If we wanted to have a picnic, we had it at the church. If we needed a job, we asked the church. If we were out of work, we talked to the church." Synagogues were the focus of Jewish life as well.

Richter's Meat Market at 676 Blair in Frogtown is only a memory today. This is how it appeared in 1905.

The need immigrants felt to settle among their own, as they faced a new language and new customs, drew them together into the distinctive neighborhoods that still exist today. They also wanted to be close to jobs in the commercial and industrial plants. As post-Civil War immigration was reaching its peak, these plants and the jobs they represented were being forced out of the downtown district and into nearby neighborhoods.

German (chiefly Austrian-Hungarian), Polish, Scandinavian and Irish laborers found homes and work in Frogtown, north of University Avenue and west of Rice Street. The origin of Frogtown's name has been lost in the mists of time. One theory holds that it refers to French settlers of the area, such as Benjamin LaFond, an early landowner who left his name on one of its streets. Another explanation attributes it to Archbishop Ireland. Standing in nearby Calvary Cemetery, the story goes, he is said to have heard the frogs croaking in a marshy area and remarked, "That sounds like a frog town." The Germans called it Froschburg, German for "Frog City."

The North End, north of the Burlington-Northern tracks and west of Jackson Street, attracted the Austrians, Germans, Hungarians, Swedes and Poles who found jobs in the railroad shops and lumber yards. Joining them by 1910 were immigrants from central Romania. The Romanians built the little St. Mary's Romanian Orthodox Church at the corner of Woodbridge and Atwater.

Graves in the Chinese section of Oakland Cemetery are a reminder of the Chinese who began arriving in the 1870s. By the 1880s, they were operating small businesses clustered on Sibley between Third and Seventh streets. Like other newcomers, the Chinese were the focus of Americanization efforts. St. Paul had a Chinese Education Society with more than thirty members in 1883; and the East Side Presbyterian Church maintained a school for the Chinese.

Italians lived on the Upper Levee or "Little Italy," a low stretch of land along the Mississippi that extended from the area near Chestnut Street to the High Bridge. Poles, Czechs, Scandinavians and Germans settled along West Seventh Street, close to jobs on the railroads and at the breweries. Community centers sprang up: the Germans' Atheneum, the Mazurka Hall of the Jewish people, and the Czechs' Czechoslovakian Protective Society, which is still standing as the C.S.P.S. Hall in the West Seventh Street neighborhood.

The Upper Levee's closely-knit Italian community was forced to relocate in the 1950s when the neighborhood was leveled.

Jobs at the railroads and breweries drew more Italians, Poles and Irish to the East Side and the neighborhoods along Payne Avenue. These neighborhoods were first settled around 1850 by Swedish immigrants, who

Helen Hinrichs and her doll in the yard of the Ferdinand Hinrichs' home, about 1900. Many well-to-do German families built homes in Dayton's Bluff.

built shanties in Swede Hollow, a ravine drained by Phalen Creek (where Edward Phelan once had a claim). The Swedes gave the name, "Svenska Dalen," to Swede Hollow. Just west of Swede Hollow is Railroad Island, a neighborhood that is completely surrounded by railroad tracks. Before the Civil War and the coming of the railroads, Railroad Island was a wealthy residential district. In the 1860s it was settled by Swedes and, later, by Irish and Italian immigrants.

During the 1880s, working class families of many ethnic groups flooded into the Lower Payne Avenue neighborhood. They built houses with the help of a local building society, and they found work among the industrial plants located south of East Seventh Street.

Dayton's Bluff — its stately homes rivaling Summit Avenue's mansions — was developed by men with such names as Burns, McLean and Wakefield. But, by the 1880s well-to-do Germans had built houses there; the homes of Ferdinand Hinrichs and Adolph Muench still stand. Other Germans, such as the Burger family, farmed fields in eastern Ramsey and Washington counties and traded at the city's easternmost commercial hub, Earl and Hudson Road.

At the crest of the bluff are the reminders of the people who preceded all others to the region surrounding what is now St. Paul. Sixteen burial mounds once crowned Dayton's Bluff; six of these remain in the forty-six-acre Mounds Park. They date from the pre-historic era of the Hopewell mound-builders — the ancestors of the Dakota people.

In the 1880s, Jewish immigrants were arriving on the West Side in great numbers from Eastern Europe and Russia. They settled first on the lower West Side "flats," the wide expanse of land that stretched from the bluffs rising above South Wabasha Street to the Mississippi. Here they took over land that had been settled earlier by French Canadian voyageurs who had retired from the declining fur trade to establish homes among a number of Dakota families who had remained there. This once was Dakota

The Alexander Ramsey House, shown here in 1900, is a museum today.

land; their village of Kaposia had existed a short way down the river. The Germans arrived in the 1850s and 1860s, and the Irish followed them. By 1910, the first of St. Paul's Mexican Americans had moved into the West Side, as the Jewish population moved out to resettle elsewhere on the West Side or in the Selby-Dale neighborhood.

St. Paul's newly wealthy — including Yankees (Henry M. Rice), Irish (James J. Hill), and Germans (Frederick K. Weyerhaeuser) — built homes along Summit Avenue. By the 1880s the Ramsey Hill neighborhood was well established within the city's social fabric. It eclipsed Dayton's Bluff and Irvine Park as the elegant residential district of St. Paul.

The movement from the old downtown district to close-in neighborhoods and eventually to suburbs beyond the city limits was possible only because of a new transportation system that, in many ways, has not since seen its equal. This was the heyday of the little yellow streetcars, the trolleys. It began with the horsecars that the St. Paul Street Railway Company set in motion in downtown St. Paul in 1872. Six of the "cracker boxes on wheels," restricted to a six-mile-an-hour speed, provided day-long service. They seated fourteen passengers; the fare was a nickel. Because the city's hills presented a problem, however, cable cars flourished briefly during the 1880s. One ran up the Selby Avenue hill, the other up East Seventh Street from Broadway to Duluth.

Although the horsecars were covering twenty miles of track by 1880, their days and those of the cable cars were numbered. By 1891, all the lines had been converted to electricity. The Selby Avenue tunnel was completed in 1907, and reduced the grade for the trolleys that ran up and down the Selby Avenue hill.

The streetcar lines helped put in place St. Paul as it is today. Suburbs that had sprung up beyond Lexington Avenue, St. Paul's western boundary until 1887, were linked to the city by both streetcars and the railroads' "short lines." Surrounded by groves of trees and rolling farmlands, real estate developments clustering around commercial cores grew into separate villages, and then expanded into city neighborhoods. Merriam Park was

Like all modern modes of transportation, streetcars had a tendency to break down. This streetcar chose to stop by the Selby Avenue tunnel. Major growth in the streetcar system was seen by the end of the nineteenth century.

established in l882, Macalester Park in 1883, St. Anthony Park in 1885, and Groveland in 1890. Throughout St. Paul, neighborhood commercial centers still exist where streetcar lines once intersected.

In their heyday around the turn-of-the-century, the interurban streetcar lines formed a network that by 1906 had spread throughout Ramsey County and into Washington and Dakota counties. Rocking along through open countryside, they brought nearby resort areas, such as White Bear Lake, within the reach of ordinary city folk. They also drew the residents of Ramsey County's historic villages — New Brighton, Roseville, Little Canada, North St. Paul and White Bear Lake — closer to the city.

By making the city's businesses, theaters, shops, and restaurants more accessible, the streetcars eased the lives of the men and women who lived in rural Ramsey County, a region that once was thick with farms. Heman Gibbs, a New England Yankee who arrived in Minnesota from Illinois in 1849, grew vegetables in what is now Falcon Heights and sold them in downtown St. Paul. His contemporary and distant neighbor, Henry Schroeder, who left Germany for America around 1875, established a dairy farm in 1884 in today's Maplewood and sold milk, butter, and cream door-to-door in St. Paul.

The trolleys provided transport for celebrations as well as daily events. When the Minnesota State Fair settled into its home on the former site of the Ramsey County Poor Farm in the Midway district, the streetcars on the Como-Harriet line brought in fair-goers from all over the Twin Cities. But the trolleys (and the fairgrounds) figured in a tragic episode, the typhoid fever epidemic that followed the outbreak of the Spanish-American War in April, 1898. When Minnesota's National Guard regiments, including six companies of St. Paul men, were mustered into service, the fairgrounds were converted into a camp.

A holiday atmosphere pervaded the camp. On one Sunday alone, more than 40,000 visitors — many of them arriving by streetcar and carrying lemonade, cakes and other homemade food — descended upon the troops.

The soldiers also spent weekends on pass in Minneapolis and St. Paul. The two cities were in the grip of their usual summer outbreak of typhoid, typically a warm-weather disease; but with the increases in population movements and additional exposure of people to each other, typhoid fever broke out in camp in just a few weeks. Investigations indicated later that the men had not only traveled to the disease and contracted it while out on pass, but that the disease also had traveled to camp by streetcar, in the food the visitors carried and in the visitors themselves as hosts for the bacillus.

With almost 500 men ill, there were not enough ambulances to transport them to city hospitals, so the streetcars that had carried the men out on pass were pressed into service. The epidemic finally abated after the troops were moved to a new campground at Fort Snelling.

Sometime later, the ST. PAUL PIONEER PRESS summed up the impact of the streetcar on St. Paul and its people:

> *"When a man can go from Arlington Hills to Merriam Park for five cents, and from the harvester works near Lake Phalen to Lake Harriet on the most distant frontier of Minneapolis territory for ten cents, he has pretty nearly achieved the maximum of comfort and economy in street railway travel... ."*

Typhoid fever swept through the Minnesota National Guard encampment at the state fairgrounds in 1898. Shown here is part of the invalid camp of the Fifteenth Minnesota Regiment after it was moved to Fort Snelling.

In 1879, telephones connected St. Paul with Minneapolis; a year later, almost 600 were in use. With neighborhoods as diverse and spread out as St. Paul's were becoming, other ways to communicate were needed. Ethnic and foreign-language newspapers flourished. French, Norwegians, Danes, Swedes, Czechs and Poles all read newspapers in their own languages — some were established as early as the 1850s. The first Norwegian language newspaper in Minnesota was published in St. Paul in 1857 and 1858. The African American community read THE APPEAL, founded in 1885, and the Jewish community read the JEWISH WEEKLY, established in 1912 and known after 1915 as the AMERICAN JEWISH WORLD.

The Germans had the greatest number of foreign-language newspapers. In 1885, 79 percent of the foreign-language newspapers throughout the United States were in German. In 1860, seven of Minnesota's fifty papers were published in German. By 1869, St. Paul had five German-language newspapers; some of them, like DER WANDERER (THE MIGRANT), were affiliated with church organizations. Over the years, St. Paul was the headquarters for more than twenty German-language papers.

Newspapers served as political forums for the city's cultural and ethnic communities. They kept readers informed on such issues as nativism (the favoring of native-born residents over immigrants), prohibition, slavery, and homestead laws. They were also a stabilizing influence for newcomers who were struggling to adjust to a new community, and they were a link to their homelands.

Reverend Edward Duffield Neill, religious leader and educator.

St. Paul's many ethnic and religious groups did not necessarily dwell any more harmoniously with each other then than they do today. Tensions, often economic in origin, allowed mistrust, suspicion, and prejudice to surface. Hostility among churches arose in the 1850s as Protestants viewed with some alarm the growth of the Catholic presence in early St. Paul. Harriet Bishop, whose Sunday School culminated in the establishment of First Baptist Church, charged that Father Ravoux was instructing Catholic children to "avoid, as a pestilence, the Protestant Sunday School." On the other hand, leaders such as Alexander Ramsey and Edward Duffield Neill sought to bring Protestantism into the public school curriculum, to legally enforce temperance and to uphold the "Protestant ethic."

The Irish, in particular, were uneasy about the presence of the African Americans who, the Irish believed, would compete for jobs. When boatloads of black laborers, headed for work at Fort Snelling, arrived in St. Paul during the Civil War, they were harassed by Irish workers at the Lower Landing. A building on Wabasha known as the "Negro rookery" was attacked in 1866 after complaints of a health hazard there. An investigation revealed that the building was "inhabited solely by negroes of all ages, sexes and shades. In one room thirteen persons were sleeping every night."

The attackers, the St. Paul Pioneer reported, "behaved in an outrageous manner, maltreating the inmates, breaking furniture, etc. The only crime of these poor people is that they are poor and live in a very humble manner, but have always been orderly and industrious. The attack on them was merely the result of a low prejudice."

The Irish community also faced prejudice. Their generosity and ready wit were overshadowed by a reputation as rough-mannered heavy drinkers. Like the Irish in the eastern United States, St. Paul's Irish gravitated toward politics. The perhaps inevitable result was that they were charged with election-rigging and bossism. Seeking the security of government jobs, Irish immigrants were particularly visible as policemen; this prompted complaints from the German population, who wanted greater representation on the force.

Even fellow Catholics were uneasy with the Irish community's political influence. Archbishop Ireland, one of the most influential of the Irish in nineteenth century Minnesota, had ardently supported the creation of a distinctively American Catholic church. He then was criticized for imposing Irish Catholic ways upon parishes. Other ethnic groups, such as the Eastern European Catholics, felt that the church's role as a social center was threatened by Irish influence.

St. Paul's Irish liked to call upon their brethren to "embrace the land, not the evil city." Archbishop Ireland was a national leader in founding rural communities for immigrants from Ireland. Most of the colonies failed, but the archbishop remained undaunted. Between 1876 and 1881, he established ten communities in five separate Minnesota counties that also provided homes for French, Belgians, Germans, English and a few Polish Catholics.

In 1880, Archbishop Ireland attempted to establish a colony in western Minnesota for poverty-stricken fishermen and garden farmers from Connemara in County Galway. The effort failed. The new settlers had no experience at growing wheat, and they had little desire to work for themselves. The failure, however, earned the archbishop additional criticism. He finally abandoned the effort and found jobs for the Connemaras in St. Paul. There they established a small settlement called "Connemara Patch," below Dayton's Bluff on Phalen Creek.

As with nearly all other immigrants to St. Paul, the Irish maintained a lively interest in their homeland. When the Fenian Brotherhood, organized in New York in 1859 to help revolutionaries in Ireland, invaded Canada in 1866, the exploit caught the interest of St. Paul's Fenians. They hatched a plot for a similar invasion in 1871. A group of thirty-five Fenians left St. Paul for a march on Canada. Their plan was to link up with Louis Riel and his *metis* and strike a blow against the British at Winnipeg. The Fenians managed to capture the Hudson's Bay Company post at Pembina before they were taken into custody by United States soldiers.

St. Paul's Jewish community had its own concerns to handle. On a summer's day in 1882, more than 200 impoverished, dirty, and hungry Jewish refugees arrived without warning at the St. Paul Union Depot, just hours before the beginning of the Sabbath. They had fled persecution in Czarist Russia, arrived in New York, and had been shipped westward without provisions or funds. The St. Paul newspapers termed this dumping of human beings "an outrage to humanity." The entire community, including the City Council and the Chamber of Commerce, came to the refugees' rescue. Funds were donated and temporary housing in a tent city was set up on the West Side.

From then on, a continuous stream of Jewish refugees quickly expanded the community. By 1900, from 4,450 to 5,000 Jews had settled in St. Paul. The older, established Jewish families — most of them from Germany — found themselves in the minority. Their social order, sense of security, way of life and matters of faith all seemed to be threatened. Lines became sharply drawn between German and Russian and Polish Jews.

Less dramatically, similar hostilities were arising between other newcomers and immigrants who were already established. In his 1912 history of St. Paul, Henry A. Castle revealed a point of view, and a prejudice that was common at that time, as he attempted to explain the clash of cultures. In a section headed "Americanizing Inferior Immigrants," Castle described the decline of the "old" immigrants who, up until 1883, had come from the British Isles, Germany, the Scandinavian countries, Holland, Belgium, France and Switzerland. By the 1880s, he wrote, more than 70 percent of the immigrants were from southern and eastern Europe and Russia.

Citing statistics from the United States Immigration Commission, Castle described the new immigrants as largely unskilled workers. About 75 percent of them were male, he wrote; about 83 percent were aged fourteen to forty-five; and 35 percent were illiterate, compared with less than 3 percent of the old immigrant class. Many of the new immigrants, he added, came without families and sent much of their earnings out of the country.

"The new immigration," Castle concluded, with obvious forboding, "coming in such large numbers, has provoked a widespread feeling of apprehension as to its effect on the economic and social welfare of the country." He saw education as important "in Americanizing this tremendous influx of foreigners. The task of assimilating the new immigration is manifestly a far greater one than that which confronted our fathers. In the matter of languages, racial traits and social environments, these newcomers are infinitely farther removed from the standards we wish them to achieve, than were our welcome kinsmen from northwestern Europe, whose transition was readily accomplished."

Castle's view was characteristic for his time, and was widely accepted among many of America's "establishment" figures. It is an irony of history that the Germans — many of whom had been firmly embedded in St. Paul's leadership since the 1850s — were viewed by men like Castle as sober, industrious workers and so, for a time, escaped the hostility and prejudice experienced by some of their fellow citizens. But, with the outbreak of

The statue of "Germania" dwarfed workmen hired to remove her on April 1, 1918. "Germania" had graced the Germania Life Insurance Building at Fourth and Minnesota.

World War I, a violent wave of anti-German hysteria was unleashed all over the country. The hostility was rooted in fear, and its victims were not just those of German birth or ancestry, but anyone who seemed to doubt the wisdom of America's entry into the war. Unlike today, the World War I period was not a time in which anti-war demonstrations, dissent, and freedom of speech were tolerated.

To monitor support for the war effort, the Minnesota Public Safety Commission was created by the legislature in 1917 and given almost dictatorial authority. While well-intentioned, the Commission was prone to issue such bulletins as this:

"It is said... that one out of every twenty persons in the nation is disloyal and about one out of every one hundred is so openly seditious that he should face a firing squad if he were to receive the sort of punishment that is meted out by any autocratic government. Anyone who talks and acts against the government in time of war...is a traitor and deserves the most drastic punishment."

The result of this proclamation was predictable. There was a rush to eliminate the study of German from the public schools. The Home Guard, formed to replace the Minnesota National Guard when it was called into service, fanned out through the neighborhoods checking draft cards and looking for "slackers." German parishes were particularly vulnerable. A German priest at Assumption Church asked the archbishop to remove eight Oblate Fathers who had recently arrived.

The statue of "Germania" on the Germania Life Insurance Company building in St. Paul was hauled down. Neighbor informed on neighbor. An avalanche of letters reporting suspicious persons poured into the Commission. Aliens were required to register. The hysteria took a ridiculous turn. Sauerkraut became "liberty cabbage," dachshunds "liberty hounds," German fried potatoes became American fries and hamburger was renamed Salisbury steak.

St. Paul Red Cross volunteers diligently rolled bandages for the troops "over there."

The war years also were characterized by an outburst of patriotic fervor. The St. Paul branch of the National Association of Patriotic Instructors was organized in March of 1917 to urge Americanization of aliens and to instruct them in patriotism. Shortly afterward, the Bohemian National Alliance and Bohemian Gymnastics Association Sokol adopted resolutions of loyalty.

Victory gardens blossomed in front and back yards. The St. Paul chapter of the American Red Cross urged women to knit socks for soldiers, and the ST. PAUL PIONEER PRESS published a pledge for women to sign in which they agreed to produce one pair of socks a week for ten weeks. Mobilization of troops in the winter of 1917-1918 brought lightless nights. Factories closed for five days to save energy. "Heatless Mondays" further limited mercantile and industrial activities. Food conservation and rationing started with wheatless and meatless days. The YWCA taught an array of new classes: how to make bread without white flour, how to make surgical dressings, how to make over clothes, even how to repair automobiles. Telegraphy classes were organized to train women to fill the jobs of men who had joined the armed forces.

Wheat flour was in short supply and sugar was rationed. However, rationing had its casualties. Just before the Armistice in 1918, the Minnesota Club was humiliated by the charge that it was hoarding sugar. In his history of the Minnesota Club in RAMSEY COUNTY HISTORY, Robert Orr Baker described the embarrassing incident:

> "A former manager, George Robinson, admitted responsibility, explaining that he felt he was acting for the welfare of the club in submitting an incorrect report on its supply of sugar. The United States Food Administration ordered the club to surrender all sugar in its possession and prohibited food brokers from supplying the club. This closed them down. For several months, the clubhouse was dark. Then Herbert Hoover, the nation's Food Administrator, lifted the ban, possibly after an appeal from some of St. Paul's Republican leaders."

Long before the community confronted the social upheavals ushered in by World War I, the women of St. Paul and Ramsey County had taken on the task of caring for others. Originally, this was accomplished through various religious organizations, such as the Sisters of St. Joseph and their founding of the first hospital in Minnesota in 1853.

In 1867, twelve women from Protestant churches — Harriet Bishop among them — laid the foundations for the Home for the Friendless. Now the Protestant Home of St. Paul, it is the oldest private home for the aged in Minnesota and is still standing as the Wilder Residence East at 753 East Seventh Street. The friendless and the homeless, many of them women with children, seemed to be everywhere in St. Paul during the years following the Civil War. They were destitute and badly nourished; many were ill or feverish with consumption (a direct contradiction to the myth of the sturdy pioneer).

The church women, now organized as the Ladies Christian Union and later renamed the Ladies Relief Association, set out to "relieve, aid, and provide Homes for the Homeless, the destitute and unfriended... ." Ethel McClure in her book, MORE THAN A ROOF, has provided a touching picture of these women at work. The need for care and shelter for the homeless was uppermost, and action by the Ladies Christian Union was prompt, she wrote. She described a day in February, 1870:

Ramsey County was one of the state's first counties to establish a "poor farm." This barn, which is on the National Register of Historic Places, was built in 1918 at the old "poor farm," now the Ramsey County Nursing Home on White Bear Avenue in Maplewood.

"Mrs. [John B.] Sanborn brought up the case of a newly arrived destitute Virginian family and it was voted to receive the mother and daughters for a time...

Mrs. Sanborn at once sent her sleigh for them and they arrived before the close of the meeting." Some months later the women agreed to "an urgent request that the Home should receive an aged Methodist minister and wife, poor, homeless and sick."

The Ladies Relief Association was joined by other organizations whose names also revealed the presence of women in the groups: The Women's Christian Association and the Women's Christian Home. The Home had begun with a request to help a sixteen-year-old girl with no family, who was existing by stealing. It was not St. Paul's first refuge for young women; the House of the Good Shepherd, a home for erring women, had been opened in 1869 by the Sisters of St. Joseph.

The government as well as the churches recognized the need to help provide for the destitute. As early as 1854, Ramsey County purchased 282 acres in Mounds View Township "to make a pauper farm." The county next bought land down the Mississippi at Pig's Eye, for a ".poor farm." Later the "poor farm" was moved to an expanse of land at Snelling and Como avenues. There it remained until 1885 when Ramsey County donated that land as the site of the Minnesota State Fair. The "poor farm" was moved to where it remains today on White Bear Avenue in Maplewood. The "farm" developed into what is now known as the Ramsey County Nursing Home. Its magnificent barn, built in 1918 and listed on the National Register of Historic Places, is a remnant of the county's rural past and of the previous century's tendency to turn to agriculture in its attempts to help the needy.

Not all of the homeless, destitute young women who were betrayed, abandoned and without family or resources were rescued. In that harsh period in history, the plight of such women could be terrifying. Some were unable to find respectable work, and many of these took another way out of poverty. "Long Kate," "Dutch Henriette" and "Mother" Robinson were three madams who managed brothels in post-Civil War St. Paul. Sociologist Joel E. Best described them in an article in RAMSEY COUNTY HISTORY.

Samantha "Long Kate" Hutton was tall and attractive. She was abandoned by her lover as a pregnant teenager and became a prostitute to survive. She arrived in St. Paul in 1867 and opened a house on Hill Street

This section of an 1888 panorama of St. Paul shows Kate Hutton's house (1) at 7 Hill Street. Henrietta Charles' house was a block away on Hill Street (2). Mary Robinson's house was located on Eighth Street between St. Peter and Wabasha (3).

a year later. "Long Kate" accumulated more than 100 vice arrests over the next fourteen years, under St. Paul's system for regulating brothel prostitution. At the age of 35 in 1881, Kate Hutton moved to the outskirts of the city, where she was shot and killed by her lover. She was buried in Oakland Cemetery.

"Dutch Henriette" was Mrs. Henrietta Charles, who was described as "stout, fat." She was born in Germany, where she is thought to have married Henry Charles, a stage driver who also was German. By 1865, they had settled in

St. Paul, where Henrietta established a brothel at 62 Washington Street — a block from Kate Hutton's. Between 1865 and 1874, Henrietta had more than sixty-five vice arrests. And like "Long Kate," her life was cut short. Henrietta died at the age of thirty-eight from "congestion of the brain," a euphemism for advanced syphilis.

Nina Clifford's establishment was located at 147 S. Washington. Nina was no longer alive when this photo was taken in 1937.

"Mother" Robinson was Mary E. Robinson, a widow who ran the city's most fashionable brothel in those early years of St. Paul's demimonde. Her house at 18 West Eighth Street was the largest and finest in St. Paul between the late 1860s and the early 1880s, when she was in business. Census records for 1870 show her owning $77,000 worth of property. Even the newspapers treated her with some respect, and she lived to retire from the business.

Like Mary Robinson, the legendary Nina Clifford was a key player in the city's vice network. Born Hanna (or Hannah) Steinbrecker, Nina Clifford apparently was a woman of style, wit and intelligence. She arrived in St. Paul in the 1880s, prospered, and built, in 1888, the city's best-known and most notorious "house of ill fame" on Hill Street.

Life for these and women like them was hazardous and often tragic. Yet it offered a way to provide for themselves, and even a step up into luxury. While they were condemned in their own time for presumed depravity, a modern view might at best concede that they had overcome formidable odds to survive.

While county governments in Minnesota accepted responsibility for some of the indigent poor, charity for the most part remained in private hands until the depression of the 1930s. In 1876, the city's first private charitable relief organization, the Society for Improving the Condition of the Poor, was founded with Henry A. Rice as president. Later renamed the Society for the Relief of the Poor, its purpose was to "give timely aid as seems most imperative, whether food, fuel...clothing and temporary financial assistance" as well as to promote "self-help...the truest charity." In 1892, the Society became part of the newly-formed Associated Charities of St. Paul which, in turn, became United Charities — the predecessor of Family Service of St. Paul. The Community Chest was founded to help support the growing array of social services. Late in the twentieth century it became the United Way.

In James J. Hill and The Opening of the Northwest, Albro Martin presents a heartwarming description of the compassion that characterized

Neighborhood House remains a vital force in the lives of West Side residents. This picture dates from the 1920s, when Neighborhood House stood at Indiana and Robertson streets, and its clientele was shifting from predominantly Jewish to Mexican American.

that period. Morgan L. Hutchins, secretary of the Society for the Relief of the Poor, traveled about St. Paul in a small, covered van pulled by an old horse. He carefully checked each appeal for help and brought deserving cases to the attention of the Society's board members. When James J. Hill, a board member, offered to replace Hutchins' old horse with a young horse, Hutchins refused. He felt, Martin wrote, that such a gift would be too out-of-keeping with the skill and tact he felt was necessary in helping people.

Through their neighborhood or settlement houses, St. Paul's cultural communities reached out to the immigrants and refugees who were flooding into the city. Because of its continued vitality, one of the best known is Neighborhood House. It has served the West Side since its founding in 1895.

Another settlement house that continues to serve the community is Merrick Community Services. It has served the East Side since 1911, when it began as Christ Child Center.

In WEST SIDE STORY II, Bill Hoffman wrote a lighthearted and loving history of Neighborhood House. It serves almost as a microcosm of the community efforts that helped immigrants adapt culturally, socially and economically to a new country. Neighborhood House began life in a converted four-flat building at 153 Robertson on the "flats." The "flats" were often flooded, but they offered refuge over the years to newcomers from so many different lands and cultures that the area became St. Paul's Ellis Island.

In the 1890s, the largest ethnic group living on the "flats" was Jewish. Their co-religionists, members of Mount Zion Temple, purchased the first building for Neighborhood House. The House later moved to the corner of Indiana and Robertson, and still later, in 1970, to a new building at 179 East Robie.

Although its early program was ecumenical, Neighborhood House was reorganized in 1903 on a nonsectarian basis. Catholics and Protestants joined with the Jewish community to hire two fulltime workers and to establish a program that would "cultivate human relationships across the lines of race and language, condition, party and creed." Its annual operations budget was $959.89.

Neighborhood House offered classes in English, clubs for boys and clubs for girls, and baseball and basketball games. Its members put on plays and held picnics. The "Workman Circle" at Neighborhood House was perhaps the first on the West Side to speak out for social causes. The Circle became a forerunner of the Loan Associations and Jewish charities.

In 1916, Hoffman wrote, the population of the "flats" was about 3,700, "plus several dozen in various stages of intoxication and debility whom the census-taker could not find." There were 650 families, with an average of almost six members each. Of these families, 582 were foreign-born; only sixty-two, or about 10 percent, had American-born parents. More than 70 percent were Jewish; 5 percent were Syrian; 5 percent were Irish; and the rest were French, Polish and other nationalities.

Typical of many American cities early in this century and particularly apparent in St. Paul was the presence of the city's leadership, with its strong sense of civic responsibility and obligations. Hoffman lists among Neighborhood House volunteers such names as Shepard, Goodkind, Ames, Dittenhofer, Severance, Tighe and Quinlan. "There is not a single name who, along with their parents and friends, did not make a considerable contribution to the life of the city," he noted.

Other changes besides the continuing influx of immigrants marked St. Paul's passage into the twentieth century. For several decades, Minneapolis and St. Paul had been engaged in a lively rivalry over transportation, urban growth, water power, agricultural resources, expansion of manufacturing, and the need for population growth. In 1880, for the first time in the history of the two cities, Minneapolis' population outdistanced St. Paul's 46,887 to 41,473.

The MINNEAPOLIS TRIBUNE announced that it expected the St. Paul newspapers to be seized with "gripes and conniptions." They were. They also were suspicious of the Minneapolis returns. As the next census rolled around, both cities were poised for the Great Census War of 1890.

St. Paul fired the opening shot on July 17, 1890, when seven

(Left) Editorial cartoonists took up the cudgel for their respective communities. The ST. PAUL GRAPHIC spoke of honor while (right) the MINNEAPOLIS TRIBUNE was more blunt. Debate sparked by the 1890 census war dominated newspapers for weeks.

FOR HER HONOR'S SAKE.
There are cases where a brother must interfere in his sister's affairs.
—St. Paul Graphic.

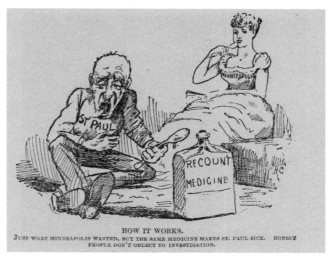

HOW IT WORKS.
JUST WHAT MINNEAPOLIS WANTED, BUT THE SAME MEDICINE MAKES ST. PAUL SICK. HONEST PEOPLE DON'T OBJECT TO INVESTIGATION.

Minneapolis census enumerators were arrested on a warrant charging fraud in counting the Minneapolis census. The hapless enumerators were hauled off to St. Paul, along with six bags of census returns. The news spread quickly. A delegation of Minneapolis citizens bailed out the enumerators; the Minneapolis newspapers were in a rage.

"It Means War!" they cried.

"The Mask of Hypocrisy Torn from the Malignant Face of St. Paul!"

The St. Paul papers shot back:

"Scheme to Swell the Population of the Flour City Knocked in the Head!" It was, the papers charged, a "villainous plot to pad the Minneapolis census by more than 100,000 names."

Subsequent investigations revealed that both cities had been flagrantly resourceful in padding their returns. St. Paul had actually been more imaginative in adding 9,425 illegal names. The enumerators had counted 325 houses that weren't on the city map; and fourteen families were listed as living in the Bank of Minnesota building, twenty-five in a hotel barber shop, 245 in the Union Depot, 120 in one small house and thirty-five in a dime museum. Minneapolis had added 18,229 illegal names, in part by including those in its cemeteries.

The United States attorney general threw out the original census and ordered a recount. The final official figures listed Minneapolis' population as 164,581 and St. Paul's as 133,156. An ironic footnote: A few years later the 1890 census forms were destroyed by a fire in Washington.

The uproar was unfortunate because the two cities were drawing together physically. The Midway district, which around the turn-of-the-century stretched from Grand Avenue on the south to the Harriet-Como streetcar line on the north, was growing. University Avenue had

James J. Hill, the "Empire Builder."

replaced the old Territorial Road and a meandering ox cart trail as a more direct route between St. Paul and Minneapolis. There was talk of a new metropolis midway between the two cities, and of a merger of Minneapolis and St. Paul. When the first state capitol burned down in 1881, Merriam Park was suggested as the location of the new capitol. About the same time, Archbishop Ireland toyed with the idea of building the new cathedral not far from his St. Paul Seminary at Cretin and Summit avenues. Both plans came to naught.

A locomotive chugged away from the Union Depot in the mid-1920s. The original depot had recently been torn down, and the current structure built in 1923.

By 1893, St. Paul had more pressing matters on its agenda. Hard times brought on by a depression created a considerable demand by the poor for assistance, especially during the winter. A year later, as the city was still in the throes of the depression, a disastrous Great Northern railway strike caused more hardship. Workers were out all along the rail line. The cause was enormous dissatisfaction over a pending wage cut, the third in less than eight months. The conflict pitted Eugene Debs, founder of the American Railway Union, against James J. Hill, the "empire builder" of the Great Northern. Confronting Hill, Debs managed a swift and dramatic victory that ended the strike after eighteen days. The workers' demands were met and Hill's trains began to roll again.

Before long, however, Hill was embroiled in one of the stormiest episodes of his life, the now legendary collision between Hill, backed by New York financier J. P. Morgan, and E. H. Harriman of the Union Pacific. Both Hill and Harriman wanted control of the Burlington Railroad through control of the Northern Pacific. Their struggle alerted President Theodore Roosevelt to the need to invoke the Sherman Antitrust Act.

The government won its antitrust suit, forcing Hill and Harriman to work out a solution. Hill retained control of his railroads, and Harriman was given a seat on the Northern Pacific and Burlington boards and on the board of the Northern Securities Company, a holding company Hill had created. The compromise, however, resulted in the federal government filing an antitrust lawsuit against Northern Securities. Both sides spent long hours testifying in St. Paul's Old Federal Courts Building, now Landmark Center. Eventually, the United States Supreme Court ordered Northern Securities dissolved.

The early years of the twentieth century were marked with change throughout the country. Cities grappled with problems created by an

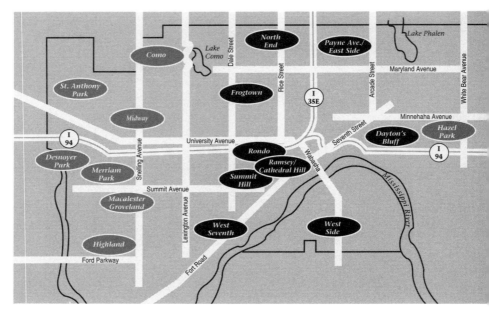

exodus by young people from rural to urban areas, and by increasing immigration of "millions of Italians, Poles, Huns and Jews who flock[ed] to America in droves every year, concentrate[ing] in the cities, and," huffed a Minneapolis banker, "creating unspeakable conditions."

The culturally diverse groups who so concerned this banker, however, often drew upon their own cultures and their tightly-knit communities as they dealt with their adjustment to America. In St. Paul, as elsewhere, newly-arrived immigrants and refugees followed a familiar pattern. They first lived in communities where there were warm ethnic and religious ties, as well as a familiar language. An example of such settlements was "Little Italy" on "the levee" in the shadow of the High Bridge. By 1900, the Irish and Polish communities that had settled there earlier were replaced almost entirely by Italians who had emigrated from two small southern Italian towns in Abruzzi-Molise. More tied to the river and more homogeneous than residents on the West Side, the community remained Italian until the 1950s. Then it was cleared by the city after repeated floods.

New social institutions appeared in St. Paul. The YWCA was founded in 1907; that same year the YMCA, founded in 1856, built a "stately ediface" at Ninth and Cedar streets. In 1911 the YWCA erected its own building at Fifth and Auditorium streets.

The problems these two organizations helped resolve were also the concerns of the Progressive movement. A major force in America's political life at this time, the Progressive movement attracted people from all political parties. Under its influence, St. Paul moved to a commission form of government in 1900, and undertook some effort at reforms. Among these efforts was a grand jury investigation in 1918 that turned up fraud in a city election.

Labor unrest continued to be typical of these years before World War I. In 1917, another disastrous strike had an immediate effect on St. Paul's residents. Streetcar motormen struck in October, stopping trolley service and setting off rioting by mobs numbering in the thousands, according to newpaper accounts.

"A score of persons were injured," the newspapers reported. "Eleven men were arrested. Scores of streetcar windows were smashed. Absolutely uncontrolled, wild crowds tied up the streetcar system of the city. Conductors and motormen were stoned from cars and ran to save themselves as the anger of the throngs vented itself on the property of the Twin City Rapid Transit Company. Stranded cars, their sides battered and their panes of glass demolished, were deserted on downtown corners. For four hours the downtown streets rang with the shouts of the mob."

The Home Guard was called out to augment Chief J. J. O'Connor's police force, and order was re-established. There was, briefly, a lighter side to the news when Louis W. Hill and a group of civic leaders revived the Winter Carnival in 1916. It had been founded in 1886 to demonstrate that St. Paul was habitable in winter, despite allegations from the East that it was not. For several decades, the carnival waxed and waned, the victim of unseasonably warm weather, financial depression, and wars; but it has been a yearly event since the end of World War II.

In the autumn of 1918, as World War I was drawing to a close, the city had to deal with another formidable foe. Spanish influenza was spreading throughout the country. Writing from Camp Grant, Illinois, Dr. Egil Boeckmann of St. Paul, a member of the State Board of Health, sounded a warning for his fellow physicians. The disease, he reported, "spreads like fire, very severe in onset and very prone to complications of Lobar Pneumonia. I want to impress upon the Board that you are dealing with the most serious epidemic of any kind you have ever been up against."

By November 1, St. Paul had 3,031 cases of influenza. Public gatherings were drastically curtailed as the disease spread, although Armistice Day brought wild crowds into the streets, spreading the disease further. Newspapers published instructions: Boil used dishes, in caring for the sick; keep linens separate; use plenty of soap and water to keep the house clean.

The City Council appointed a Citizens' Committee, chaired by Louis W. Hill, to establish a special influenza hospital. Face masks were advised and even became a fashion fad; a group of Summit Avenue women created a sensation by wearing chiffon veils as masks to a tea. The St. Paul Gas Light Company asked the Citizens' Committee for 1,500 masks for its employees and American Hoist and Derrick also requested 1,500 masks.

The epidemic finally abated as the first two decades of the twentieth century drew to a close. New issues would rise to the surface as the Roaring Twenties began, and St. Paul's cultural diversity would be enriched by the growth of the Mexican American settlement and the flowering of the African American community.

PART IV:

DECADES OF CHANGE
1920 – 1950

As the 1920s began, some of the great social movements of the twentieth century — women's suffrage, prohibition, and social service — were in place. The freeing of women from the straight-laced Victorian concept of the True Woman was accelerated by World War I but had begun years earlier when women began to leave their homes for service in the community.

Community groups were active in support of the World War I effort. The Junior League was selling flowers for the "Soldier's Club Flower Sale" across from Rice Park.

In St. Paul, women established public drinking fountains throughout the city. They organized Children's Health Days and provided fresh milk for children through milk stations they set up in the schools. They framed laws that would protect women and children, and they lobbied for the laws. They founded Mothers' Clubs that evolved into the schools' Parent-Teacher Associations. They taught Americanization classes, and they taught poorer women how to sew. They worked in the Red Cross during the first World War, and they turned out fearlessly to tend the injured and the homeless during such disasters as the Moose Lake forest fire.

Women accomplished much of this as active community volunteers, but many also held fulltime jobs. They were lawyers, business owners, physicians, teachers, writers, entrepreneurs, policewomen, real estate agents, stock brokers, artists and actresses, government employees and politicians, and they assumed many other responsibilities women had seldom assumed. Their cultural backgrounds were diverse — German, Swedish, Norwegian, Irish, African American, Jewish — but most of them shared a passionate devotion to the cause of women's suffrage.

Carrie Haskins Backus founded the St. Paul school for girls that for many years bore her name. She organized the Thursday Club, several study clubs for women, lectured on Shakespeare, and was state secretary of forestry for the Minnesota Federation of Women's Clubs. Katherine Louise Dunn Slater, also a teacher, took over her husband's insurance business when he was called into service in World War I. She was secretary of the first Minnesota State Parent-Teacher Association.

Ellen and Eliza Ireland and Ellen Howard, who joined the Sisters of St. Joseph, helped establish St. Joseph's Academy. They also established and built Minnesota's first arts school, St. Agatha's Conservatory, which is still standing as the Exchange Building at Cedar and Exchange streets in downtown St. Paul. Ellen and Eliza Ireland were the sisters of Archbishop John Ireland; Ellen Howard, who became Sister Celestine, was their cousin. Ellen Ireland became Sister Seraphine, then Mother Seraphine, the province superior; Eliza Ireland became Sister St. John.

Minnie Fay Hession was a St. Paul policewoman. After her appointment in 1913, she worked with domestic problems, inspected dance halls, helped runaway girls and found homes for unmarried pregnant women. Mary Frances Kordosky was the first woman to serve as deputy sheriff of Ramsey County. Before her appointment in 1923, she bought, furnished and sold apartment buildings, and worked as a railroad inspector. German-born Laura Dussair Gloeser was the first matron of the Ramsey County jail and the county's first visiting nurse.

Nellie Griswold Francis, Esther Frankel, Mary Handran Hurley, Harriet Warner Schoonmaker and Mable Hansen Guise were community activists. Nellie Francis was the author of the anti-lynching bill that passed the 1920-1921 state legislature. She was president of the Minnesota State Federation of Colored Women and editor of TRI-CITY AGE, its official publication. Esther Frankel was active in the Council of Jewish Women. She helped persuade the St. Paul School Board to install penny lunches at Lafayette School, and she established a vocational training school for the blind.

Mary Hurley was the first woman to be elected to the St. Paul Board of Control, as well as serving as overseer for Ancker Hospital. Harriet Schoonmaker was secretary of Minnesota's Minimum Wage Commission. Mabel Guise successfully lobbied the legislature to allow women to serve on juries and to establish a fifty-four hour work week for women in industry.

Anne Egan Forrestal was appointed deputy collector of the Internal Revenue Service in 1922. Before her appointment, she had been executive secretary of the Ramsey County League of Women Voters and the Republican Women's Club. In 1922, Else Redeker Obst became the first woman to be elected treasurer of Ramsey County.

Clara Linz Bermeier was the publisher of the St. Paul German-language newspaper, the DAILY VOLKS ZEITUNG. She took over the newspaper

*(Top)
Sister Seraphine
in later years
as Mother
Seraphine.
(Middle)
Carrie Haskins
Backus, school
founder.
(Bottom)
Grace Flandrau,
popular author.*

after the death of her husband, its founder. For eighteen years she managed it and other semi-weekly and semi-monthly papers, including the RIVERSIDE PRESS. Eliza Thompson Edgerton Newport established a houseboat at the Lower Landing that was the first in America to offer inexpensive clean lodgings for working men. She also founded the first coffee house to sell food at cost in St. Paul. Sophie Greve Kenyon was a stockbroker for thirty years. She also organized the Woman's Welfare League, the first large suffrage club in Minnesota.

Grace Hodgson Flandrau was a writer, known nationally for two novels, COUSIN JULIA and BEING RESPECTABLE, and for many short stories published in MCCLURES, HARPERS, THE SATURDAY EVENING POST, and other magazines. Julie Celina Gauthier was a portrait painter who also taught art in St. Paul high schools.

Many women influenced St. Paul through their membership in the Women's Christian Temperance Union (WCTU), which had an active franchise section. Liquor continued to be as much of a problem after the turn-of-the-century as it had been in frontier St. Paul and it was of great concern to these women as they saw the effect of alcohol on families whose wage earners spent their pay checks at the corner saloon.

Without an understanding of alcoholism (sometimes called dipsomania) as an incurable disease, these women turned to other remedies. Margaret Walsh Kelly, Irish-born and one of St. Paul's first policewomen, was president for years of the Sacred Thirst Total Abstinence Society and active in the Catholic Total Abstinence Union of America. Her influence extended beyond the alcohol problem. She drew up an ordinance regulating public dancing. Emma Elizabeth Armstrong was Ramsey County superintendent of moral education for the WCTU, as prohibition waited in the wings in 1917 and 1918. Eva Jones founded the Minnesota WCTU, then devoted the rest of her life to working with the WCTU in St. Paul. When she died in 1914, the Ramsey County WCTU erected a memorial fountain in her honor in Rice Park.

Eva Jones, founder of the Minnesota Women's Christian Temperance Union.

A new community playground movement that promoted the "wholesome influence of family life" captured the interest of other St. Paul women. The city's playgrounds grew out of this. Florence Elfelt Bramhall's efforts with the Women's Civic League resulted in the revision of the city charter that provided for playgrounds and their support. By 1912, St. Paul had eighty playgrounds, parks, squares and boulevards. They were created as part of the "city beautiful" effort that swept the country as once-raw frontier villages

prospered, matured, and turned from the necessities to the amenities.

St. Paul's first parks had been set aside as early as 1849, before the creation of New York's Central Park. Smith (now Mears), Rice and Irvine Parks at first were simply open spaces with trees, where cows grazed and women hung laundry. As the city developed, so did its parks. Horace W. S. Cleveland, the Chicago landscape architect, visited

St. Paul in 1872 and proposed the creation of a city-wide park system. A board of park commissioners was formed in 1884 and the move to establish more major city parks was underway. In 1873, Como Park was created when the city bought the lake and the surrounding land for $100,000; the conservatory was built in 1915. Acquisition of land for Phalen Park was completed in 1899 at a cost of $22,000 and the park soon was opened to the public.

Other major parks established early in this century, including Central, Summit, Park Place and Lafayette, have since disappeared. Others, such as Hampden and Carpenter parks, are almost forgotten. Still others have been greatly changed.

Harriet Island was once described as "covered by shade trees and always tempered by the cool breezes of the river." It had "one of the most superb public baths in the country," used by almost 1.5 million patrons over one six-year period. There was a beach where people swam in the Mississippi until pollution of the water put a stop to the practice; and there

(Top) Irvine Park was the centerpiece for its surrounding neighborhood in the early 1900s. It set a standard for the many city parks and playgrounds established at that time. (Bottom) The once beautiful LaFayette Park had to make way for downtown development.

Harriet Island's bathing beach gained citywide prominence, thanks to the efforts of Dr. Justus Ohage. Ohage, the city public health officer, was instrumental in the development of the island.

were refreshment pavilions, outdoor picnic grounds, playgrounds and a zoo, until repeated flooding forced the removal of Harriet Island's menagerie to Como Zoo. In an interesting contemporary note, there was a free day nursery where working mothers could leave their children.

For some, the Jazz Age — the Roaring Twenties — was a prosperous time. Among St. Paul's African Americans, it was a period of economic progress before the setbacks brought on by the Great Depression of the 1930s. The city's African American community had, for almost forty years, been the social and cultural center for all blacks in Minnesota, although by the 1920s it was being overshadowed by the community in Minneapolis.

Although St. Paul's black community was fairly well established by 1910, its history dated back more than seventy years to the time when James Thompson helped build the Market Street Methodist Church and became the only black member of the Old Settlers Association. By 1848, thirty-five black men and women had settled in Minnesota — most of them in St. Paul. Twenty years later, the state legislature granted African American men the right to vote, two years before the nation as a whole adopted the Fifteenth Amendment to the Constitution. In 1898, Minnesota passed a civil rights bill that guaranteed protection from discrimination based on race, color, religion or national origin. It was introduced by J. Frank Wheaton, an 1894 graduate of the University of Minnesota's Law School and the state's first black legislative representative.

Although African Americans settled first around the Lower Landing in downtown St. Paul, by 1920 most had moved out of the downtown district. Some crossed the river to the West Side "flats" and found work with the packing plants, such as Armour and Swift in South St. Paul; some moved to the neighborhood near the state capitol; and some migrated to the district west of Summit Avenue that was being vacated by the German Jews as they moved to Highland Park.

The neighborhood lying between Marshall and University, Dale and

Rice streets, was disrupted by urban renewal and the construction of Highway 94 in the 1960s, but the now-vanished Rondo Street once ran through its heart. Here African Americans established a community filled with business and professional men and women, scholars and entrepreneurs. These resourceful achievers served both as role models and employers for other blacks. They also remained an integral part of the work forces of the railroads that had made St. Paul an important rail center.

In his history of St. Paul's African American community, published in RAMSEY COUNTY HISTORY, Arthur C. Mc Watt described how the black press also played an important role in motivating the black community and knitting it together. THE APPEAL, edited by John Quincy Adams, kept a vigilantly watchful eye out for racist barbs in other local newspapers, and for transgressions against black citizens. A militant and outspoken Republican, Adams expanded publication of THE APPEAL into Dallas, Washington, D. C., St. Louis, Louisville, Chicago and Minneapolis, as well as St. Paul. At one time, the paper also had correspondents in Denver, Des Moines and Milwaukee.

Owen Howell bought THE APPEAL in 1924, after Adams' death. With a young Roy Wilkins, Howell began publishing the ST. PAUL ECHO. Mc Watt described how Howell urged fiscal solidarity upon the community. In his first issue, Howell noted that although "the 1,200 colored families of St. Paul spend approximately $40,000 annually on milk, our black papers still have no ads from white milk companies, nor do they hire any colored drivers. We spend $50,000 on laundry, yet there are no ads or colored drivers. It would seem only a boycott would change the picture."

In 1926, Roy Wilkins also reminded readers that, "if all our colored families would spend just one dollar a week with the two colored grocery stores, they would make $24,000 a year. If Negroes buy

Frederick McGhee, the first African American criminal lawyer west of the Mississippi, lived in this house at 665 University Avenue. He was active in opening up employment opportunities for blacks.

from Negroes, then Negroes have the money and the goods, too. This is the right road to race economic security." Another effective African American leader, Mc Watt noted, was Frederick L. McGhee. A prominent Democrat and a Catholic, McGhee was the first black criminal lawyer west of the Mississippi. He used his considerable influence at city hall to open up employment opportunities for blacks, helping them find jobs as policemen and fire fighters.

St. Paul's black leaders explored a variety of routes to financial security, often at the same time. T. H. Lyles was a leading businessman who ran one of St. Paul's finest barber shops and also worked as a mortician and a realtor. His wife was a versatile businesswoman who operated the Hair Bazaar on East Third Street. It offered ladies' baths, shampoos and hairstyling, but the shop also sold and rented masquerade costumes, mourning clothes, and wedding attire.

Lyles was succeeded as the city's leading black entrepreneur by Howell. Besides publishing the Echo, Howell opened a Valet Tailoring Service in 1920 at Fifth and Wabasha. Other entrepreneurs, Mc Watt wrote, were H. H. Kent, who had a delivery and forwarding company on West Seventh Street and also hired out his wagons and excursion buses; and O.C. Hall and his brother, S. E. (Ed) Hall, who operated the Hall Brothers Barber Shop. The Halls also ran an informal and ingeniously organized job placement service out of their shop. They relied on tips from the black community and other clientele, and they worked with Thomas Morgan, who printed The Helper and advertised the job openings.

Through the years, the African American community's professional men included physicians, dentists, architects, engineers, educators and clergymen. T. C. Cuthbert, a civil engineer, founded the St. Paul Paving and Construction Company, one of the largest black-owned businesses in St. Paul. He employed nineteen black masons and laborers.

Dr. Valdo Turner, a graduate of the Meharry Medical School, served on the staff of St. John's Hospital in St. Paul; he was a founder of the St. Paul chapter of the National Association for the Advancement of Colored People (NAACP). Dr. Thomas S. Cook was the first African American physician to pass the Minnesota Board of Medical Examiners in 1899. Dr. J. Walton Crump, a University of Iowa graduate, arrived in St. Paul in 1924. He was the first black physician to be admitted to the Ramsey County Medical Association and one of the first from the Midwest to become a member of the American Medical Association. Dr. Earl Weber, a dentist, was a graduate of the University of Minnesota's School of Dentistry.

John Henry Hickman, son of pioneer clergyman Robert Hickman, was the first Minnesota-born African American to graduate from the St. Paul (now William Mitchell) College of Law, Mc Watt noted, and James P. Anderson, another graduate, became the first black to practice before the Minnesota Supreme Court. Leona O. Smith was the only black woman attorney in St. Paul. In 1927, she became deputy regional director of the National Bar Association, founded to serve members of the African American legal profession who were excluded from membership in the American Bar Association.

Dr. Valdo Turner was one of St. Paul's earliest African American physicians. His office, shown here, was located at 27 E. 7th St.

Clarence Wigington, a bright young architectural draftsman, worked for the St. Paul Parks, Playgrounds and Public Buildings Department. He drafted the plans for the Homecroft and Hazel Park school, for the Highland Park Water Tower near Snelling Avenue and Ford Parkway, and for other public buildings. Later, as a private architect, he drew the plans for the St. James A.M.E. Church.

Attorney W. T. Francis helped his wife and other community leaders successfully lobby the state legislature into passing the first anti-lynching bill in the United States. Their efforts followed the lynching in 1920 in Duluth of three black circus employees accused of raping a white woman. Francis later became United States consul to Liberia.

While many of St. Paul's African Americans achieved success, there still were countless barriers. Clerical and white collar jobs remained scarce. Dwight Reed, Sr., an electrical engineer, had to take a job as street gang foreman for the city's black paving crews. New organizations were established as the community continued to help itself. The St. Paul Negro Business League, formed in 1922, promoted black businesses. The Pullman Porters Industrial Association, forerunner of the Pullman Porter Brotherhood, met for the first time in St. Paul in 1922. The St. Paul Urban League was organized in 1923. The St. Paul chapter of the NAACP, the oldest civil rights organization in the country, had been organized back in 1913. (Roy Wilkins would rise to national prominence as its head from 1955 to 1977.)

Three community centers were serving African American families: Neighborhood House on the West Side "flats"; Welcome Hall at St. Anthony and Farrington, which offered the black community its first day-care center; and the Hallie Q. Brown Center, which opened in 1929 in the Union Hall at Aurora and Kent streets. The Hallie Q. Brown Center was named for the nationally-known educator, lecturer and author.

In 1927, Mc Watt wrote, Roy Wilkins told his ECHO readers that:

"The colored people of St. Paul live in one of the city's best locations. It is near the downtown shopping area, it is convenient to both cities...it has its streets well-lined with beautiful trees... ." Wilkins described Rondo Street as it once was, and as it has remained in many people's memories: "...a riot of warm colors, feeling and sounds.... Music is in abundance from victrolas, saxophones, player pianos and hurry-up orchestras which pour out their complaints to the passing scene. It seethes with the pulsating beauty of the lives of its people who feel intensely every emotion which stirs their being."

Despite the euphoria and the sense that good times would never end, which suffused the 1920s, Wilkins was writing in the midst of one of the worst crime eras in St. Paul's history. Those realists who had predicted that the American people would never accept the outlawing of liquor were proved absolutely correct. Prohibition, that national experiment President Hoover called "noble in intent," ushered in a period of lawlessness and corruption that held the entire nation in its grip.

Half the people in the country, it was said, were making home brew. In St. Paul, hundreds of speakeasies opened up — some of them downtown where they did a thriving noon-hour business. The Green Lantern, a bar and supper club at 545-1/2 Wabasha Street, was a favorite. Other popular spots included the Green Dragon Restaurant at Snelling and University, the

Boulevards of Paris at Lexington and University, the Brown Derby at Seven Corners, the Plantation at White Bear Lake, the Hollywood Club at the east end of the Mendota bridge, and the Hollyhocks, a spacious three-story house surrounded by a veranda on Mississippi River Drive, north of West Seventh Street.

Prostitution and gambling flourished along Jackson and St. Peter streets and around Seven Corners. Violence was common. Two men and a woman were shot down not far from the state capitol in what the newspapers called "the third outbreak of gang warfare in the Twin Cities within two weeks."

It was clear to police and federal agents that by 1925 crime syndicates had moved into the bootlegging business. Word of the O'Connor system spread through the underworld. This was an agreement devised by Chief of Police John J. O'Connor and his brother, Richard, that criminals would not be arrested in St. Paul if they obeyed the law.

The O'Connor system, however, was not just a response to the crime wave of the 1920s. This scheme for controlling criminals had been operating since the turn-of-the-century in St. Paul. It also demonstrated the political power of the city's Irish and German voters. As Ann Regan noted in THEY CHOSE MINNESOTA, all but one of the ten men who served as St. Paul mayors between 1932 and 1972 had Irish surnames. In 1920, she wrote, eleven of the twelve members of the State Democratic Committee were Irish — enough Irish, the ST. PAUL PIONEER PRESS commented, "to make up a creditable ball team," with the sole non-Irishman as umpire.

Irish dominance of the Democratic party in St. Paul dated all the way

((Left) Fighting "demon rum" and other spirits took many forms. Stills were dismantled, vats smashed and liquor dumped on the ground. (Right) Chief of Police John J. O'Connor, of "O'Connor System" notoriety.

Irish control of St. Paul's political system was frequently lampooned in editorial cartoons. Note the "Democratic pup on tap" in the background.

back to the 1850s when William Pitt Murray, a Scotch-Irish lawyer, joined with Louis Robert, the French trader, to control city politics. At the turn-of-the-century, Richard T. O'Connor, known as "the Cardinal," and Police Chief John O'Connor, called "the Big Fellow," were the city's political leaders. For twenty years they were allied with the businessmen of the city, such as James J. Hill and brewers William Hamm, Sr., and Otto Bremer.

The O'Connor system worked for awhile. Vice was kept under control by the simple expedient of extracting "fees" periodically for allowing it to flourish. Consequently, for years reported crime rates remained low. Inevitably, however, the system broke down. The O'Connor brothers retired from local politics, the 1920s ended with the stock market crash in 1929, prohibition was repealed in 1933, profits from bootlegging vanished and organized crime turned to bank robbery and kidnapping.

After his release by kidnappers, William Hamm, Jr., met the press outside of the family home.

By the early 1930s, St. Paul was in the midst of a major crime spree. On August 30, 1933, Swift and Company's $30,000 payroll was seized in South St. Paul. In the shoot-out, buildings for two blocks around were sprayed with machine gun bullets, a policeman was killed and another injured. In the wave of kidnappings, Haskell Bohn, son of the founder of Bohn Refrigeration Company in the Midway district, was kidnapped. Political boss and bootlegger Leon Gleckman was seized outside his suite in the St. Paul Hotel. Brewer William Hamm, Jr., was forced into a car at Greenbrier and Minnehaha. Banker Edward Bremer was seized at Goodrich and Lexington on his way to work.

All were released after ransoms were paid, but St. Paul's powerful families, afraid they might be the next victims, were in a state of panic. They appealed for help from Washington, where officials labeled the city a "hotbed of crime, poison spot of the nation, a haven for criminals, a citadel of crime." Newspapers across the country attacked St. Paul as "a protected city" that invited "scores of big-time crooks to make St. Paul their hang-out."

On the same day that John Dillinger and his gang shot their way out of an apartment at Lincoln and Lexington avenues, a blue-ribbon grand jury probing charges of lax law enforcement concluded that there was "no justification for any charges that an excess of crime exists here." Nevertheless, orders went out to clean up the city. Gambling joints and houses of prostitution were closed, slot machines picked up, and liquor licenses revoked. The police force also cleaned house. The F.B.I. shot and killed Dillinger in Chicago. Alvin Karpis, leader of the Barker-Karpis gang, was arrested in 1936 and, after a trial in St. Paul's Old Federal Courts Building, was convicted of the Hamm and Bremer kidnappings.

In retrospect, the 1920s and early 1930s were a colorful period in St. Paul's history, but there were dark overtones. These would deepen as the depression clamped down on the country.

As the problems of city life continued to develop in an expanding St. Paul, a new community was establishing itself. Mexican Americans had begun to arrive in greater numbers in St. Paul between 1912 and 1916, and immigration continued in increasing numbers during the 1920s and 1930s. By 1936, most of the Mexicans who had migrated to St. Paul were American citizens, and most were from the southwestern United States; some had emigrated legally from Mexico. They were workers in Minnesota's sugar beet industry — recruited by the industry when it faced chronic labor shortages due to World War I and the immigration quotas of the 1920s. When the seasonal work in the fields ended, many of the Mexican workers remained in Minnesota over the winter. They found work as laborers on the railroads in St. Paul or in South St. Paul packing plants. Some of the Mexicans settling in St. Paul were illegal immigrants who had entered the

Swede Hollow, born out of shanties scattered along Phalen Creek, was home to Swedes, Irish, Poles, Italians, and Mexican Americans before it was razed in the 1950s.

United States either "dry" (by crossing the Arizona or New Mexico borders) or "wet" (by wading the Rio Grande).

The Mexican American community was the last of St. Paul's newcomers to find shelter in Swede Hollow. They also settled on the low land under the Third and Sixth Street bridges; north of the city market around Jackson and East Fifteenth Street; and on the West Side "flats." The heart of their community was located at Fairfield, State and Indiana streets. There, in this Ellis Island of St. Paul, the Mexican Americans dwelt in reasonable harmony with the Eastern European Jews, who were beginning to leave for Highland Park, the African Americans and at least twenty other ethnic groups.

Living in the worst housing in St. Paul at that time, the Mexican Americans, the "poorest of the poor," had one of the lowest crime rates in the city. Their cultural and social life centered around Our Lady of Guadalupe Church, with its clubs and special programs, and Neighborhood House with its English and citizenship classes, social clubs, and employment counseling.

In 1933, Neighborhood House was reaching only about half of the Mexican Americans in St.

Mexican Americans became the dominant Neighborhood House clients by the 1930s. This group of children enjoyed playing in a band.

Paul; five years later it was reaching nearly all of them (seven-eighths). Its importance in the lives of the people it served was summed up by one Mexican American mother:

> "Neighborhood House has been so good to me and my family. We come from Texas. My husband he works for packing company. Neighborhood House help get him job. Neighborhood House teach he and I to speak American. Neighborhood House make us citizens of United States, help us get start here. At Neighborhood House I learn to sew and cook American way. My children go there, too. Ever since they very small they learn and play at Neighborhood House. Never have to worry if they there. Neighborhood House know American way — help us teach our children right. Neighborhood House my first real friend here."

Our Lady of Guadalupe Church was a bridge to the future for these lower West Side Mexican immigrants. The church was established as a mission in 1931 with the help of the Guild of Catholic Women. Guild members had become concerned about the plight of their fellow Catholics among the Mexicans on the West Side. A history of the Guild describes the founding of the mission:

"The Guild opened a refuge in a vacant store on South Wabasha. The owner agreed to a lease of $25 a month, or improvements up to a value of $300 on the property. The latter terms were agreed to and the lease was signed in the name of the Guild. This dingy grocery store was transformed into a chapel. Within six weeks $1,400 had been donated, along with an organ given to the mission by the Polish church."

The first priest of Our Lady of Guadalupe was Joseph Guillmette of St. Thomas College (now the University of St. Thomas). He set up depots where food and clothing could be donated, and he spent much of his time caring for the desperate needs of his people. A little more than a year later, the church expanded into part of a building that also housed a tavern and pool hall. In 1939, the entire building was purchased and the church was incorporated as a parish. Later, the church was enlarged and a parish hall was built.

News of the stock market crash in 1929 caused a run on banks throughout the city. In 1933, more news of financial calamity prompted this run on First National Bank.

Like many other groups of immigrants, Mexican Americans are enriched with a legacy of customs from the past that are still observed today. Mexican Americans from throughout St. Paul gather on the West Side to celebrate *Cinco de Mayo* (the Fifth of May) and *El Grito* (the Cry), festivals that mark Mexican independence days, and *El Dieciseis di Setiembre* (the Sixteenth of September), the harvest festival.

Homeless, jobless men sleeping on park benches were a familiar sight during the depression.

A sad-faced woman found some warmth from a pot-bellied stove.

St. Paul's African Americans never completely shared in the prosperity of the 1920s, and the Mexican Americans even less. Both groups suffered serious problems during the depression of the 1930s. The depression began in the wake of the terrible Black Tuesday, October 29, 1929, and the crash of the stock market after almost a month of near collapse and panic selling. For the first time in history, brokerage houses in St. Paul were crowded until long after dark. Outside the Western Union office in the Pioneer building, crowds of worried men milled about as the latest stock quotations were posted in the windows.

The depression that followed was the worst economic turn-down in American history. It was a period of national tragedy, as well as a world-wide economic debacle. By 1932, there were 15,000 men out of work in St. Paul — one out of every five families. The St. Paul Association of Commerce had assured President Hoover that the city would care for its own, but the mounting relief roles overwhelmed St. Paul's strong network of private charities. Homeless and jobless men slept in the city's parks and went door to door through the residential districts seeking a meal from compassionate housewives. The April 11, 1934 edition of the St. Paul Daily News described how two destitute men made their home in Carver's Cave. They sold crafts, including latticework and baskets, to eke out a living.

A. A. Heckman, the dean of Minnesota's social workers, remembered public welfare in Ramsey County at that time as "one person sitting on a high stool behind a wicker grill [in the courthouse]...passing out orders for groceries...In the winter, coal occasionally was provided to needy families. However, there was nothing provided for clothing, utilities or rent." Louis W. Hill, independently and secretly, bought a train load of food that he stored in a warehouse and in a cave under the bluff below Kellogg Boulevard. With Heckman's help, this was parceled out to desperate families.

Private efforts, however, by individuals or groups were not enough. Desperately needed assistance finally arrived in the form of the federal

Surplus food was distributed to St. Paul families in 1934. Dried milk also was given away.

relief program, the New Deal organized under President Franklin D. Roosevelt in 1933. The program was a move that marked a fundamental change in social policy: The government entered into the welfare business and remained there. Never again would the country rely entirely upon private funds to help the poor and the disadvantaged.

Relief efforts were community-wide and involved the city's business and political leadership: Frederick R. Bigelow, of St. Paul Fire and Marine; Julian Baird and Richard Lilly of First National Bank; attorney William Mitchell of Doherty, Rumble and Butler; Rabbi H. S. Margolis of Mount Zion Temple; Homer Clark of West Publishing Company; Horace Kline of Webb Publishing Company; Frederick Crosby and Harold Washburn of American Hoist and Derrick; and George Sommers of G. Sommers and Co.

Memories of those years are vivid. A "moat" — a depressed sidewalk — encircled the Ramsey County courthouse where the county welfare board had its office. People seeking relief often filled it, standing four abreast in a line that extended down Wabasha for two blocks. They were waiting for small $5 and $10 grocery vouchers. Heckman remembered seeing men pacing up and down outside the Wilder Building, where private relief agencies had offices, trying to gather the courage to come in and apply for relief.

For the African Americans and the Mexican Americans, the work programs of the New Deal should have helped stem a slide into unemployment. Although by the mid-1930s St. Paul had a substantial black business community of small stores, shops, restaurants, bars and barber shops, lack of money often forced them to close their doors. Black lawyers, doctors and dentists stayed afloat only because of white clients. Blacks too often were the last hired and first fired on many jobs. The eleven railroads operating out of St. Paul laid off black Pullman porters, red caps, and other workers. Only the black postal workers enjoyed some measure of financial security.

The federal relief programs were of some help, but David V. Taylor points out in They Chose Minnesota that,

"Discrimination seems to have been pervasive in the administration, in the placement of persons on government-sponsored projects, and in

The Works Progress Administration provided jobs as well as a wide variety of other opportunities for the city's residents. Mexican Americans made up this WPA English class.

working conditions." In May, 1938, he wrote, a St. Paul Urban League speaker reported "that approximately 69 percent of the city's blacks were either on direct relief or participating in such federal help programs as the Civilian Conservation Corps (CCC) or the Works Progress Administration (WPA)."

The Mexican Americans who had been brought into Minnesota during the boom years were almost entirely displaced by white workers during the depression. Because the major source of employment, even for those Mexican Americans living in St. Paul, continued to be seasonal work in the beet fields, they were encouraged to continue in these jobs in an effort to reduce the drain on county relief agencies. However, they faced competition from workers who were flooding into Minnesota from other states. A 1936 survey revealed that out of 1,791 beet workers living in Ramsey County, 1,761 were on relief. Many Mexicans also feared deportation as a way of removing them either from the job market or the relief rolls. St. Paul had the dubious distinction of being one of the first major cities in the United States to deport Mexicans. Of the 324 people deported in 1934, most were children, and of the adults, some were, indeed, United States citizens.

WPA and PWA programs provided only slight relief for Mexican Americans, who often had difficulty meeting residency requirements and lacked skills that could qualify them for work outside the beet fields. Prejudice also played a large role. In 1938, two years after the 1936 survey, a new survey indicated that 168 Mexican American families out of 259 living in Ramsey County were on relief and only twenty-five held WPA jobs.

In summing up the struggles of the 1930s among those living on the West Side, Bill Hoffman perhaps spoke for all of St. Paul's people in his TALES OF HOFFMAN:

"These were the proud and stubborn people...who labored valiantly to hide their despair and fear of unemployment from their neighbors and from their children. Real money was scarce, but when had there been plenty?"

In 1939, with the outbreak of war in Europe, a cautious call-up of reserves began in the United States. The nation was preparing itself for the second major war of the twentieth century. The 18th Infantry Battalion, a Marine Reserve ground unit activated in St. Paul, was sent to Iceland. A group of St. Paul men who belonged to the 47th Naval Reserve Division of the 11th Battalion was called up and assigned to an overage destroyer, the U.S.S. WARD, on duty in Hawaiian waters.

On the morning of December 7, 1941, the WARD was patrolling off the channel entrance to Pearl Harbor. Nine of the St. Paul men were manning a four-inch gun mounted on top of the ship's galley deck house. About 6 a.m., shortly before the first Japanese dive-bombers rounded Diamond Head, the WARD saw something in the water and closed to investigate. It was a midget enemy submarine attempting to slip through the net guarding the harbor. The gun crew fired and sank the submarine. It was the first American shot of World War II. The WARD was sunk later during the battle for the Philippines, but its gun had been removed. Today the gun is mounted on the capitol grounds in St. Paul as a monument to the Minnesota men who fought in the second World War.

Within days following the Japanese attack on Pearl Harbor, St. Paul was on a war footing as young men lined up at the armed forces recruiting offices in the Old Federal Courts Building. The hysteria that characterized World War I was absent in St. Paul, but sabotage was considered a threat. The army asked that Mississippi River Boulevard be closed off to protect the Ford Motor Company, which had begun to manufacture armored vehicles. Flights from three airports near the Twin City Ordnance

(Top) This wartime job training and job safety display encouraged the local work force. (Bottom) PFC Gladys Anderson and Pvt. Albert Larson joined other couples in wartime marriages. She was stationed in Washington, D.C. and he was at Fort Lewis, Washington.

Vern Soash of Minnesota Federal handed out badges to LaFayette School students who had purchased one war stamp per week for six weeks in 1943.

Plant of the Federal Cartridge Corporation at New Brighton were restricted. Bridges over the Mississippi were patrolled.

Air raid wardens paced St. Paul's streets; air raid shelters were set up. Rationing of food, fuel, and shoes went into effect. Restaurant owners complained that they couldn't get enough food to feed the influx of customers who were eating out to supplement rationed food at home. Once again, victory gardens blossomed all over the city. An additional 300 streetcars were put into service to handle the extra rush-hour riders that gas rationing created.

If opportunity can arise out of tragedy, it did so as a rather un-expected result of World War II. Men and women from all of St. Paul's culturally diverse communities served in the armed forces. Many who came home participated in post-war G.I. benefits. Those who had to remain behind found jobs and, often for the first time, some measure of financial security as a result of the war-induced labor shortages. At least seventeen war plants were operating in the Twin Cities metropolitan region. This gave a significant boost to opportunities for both skilled and professional workers, and particularly for women, African Americans and Mexican Americans. Thousands of women were at work in the cities' war plants. At Holman Field, where a bomber modification center was established, more than 5,000 men and women installed such special equipment as bombsights on military aircraft that were flown in from around the country. Many of the pilots ferrying the planes were women.

More than 1,000 African American workers were employed at the Twin City Ordnance Plant at New Brighton. Arthur Mc Watt described how Charles Horn, who managed the plant, brought in Cecil Newman, editor of the St. Paul Recorder, as advisor to the supervisor of industrial relations, and later as director of Negro personnel.

"Over the next few years, Newman placed blacks in more than forty job categories," Mc Watt wrote in Ramsey County History. "Before the war, they had been restricted to fewer than a dozen categories. These opportunities, along with many new job openings which had been created by the draft and war labor shortages, gave African American job seekers a chance to learn new skills which later translated into new business and marketing initiatives."

The G.I. bill, Mc Watt added, gave significant numbers of blacks professional training for the first time. "It was," he said, "truly a take-off period in St. Paul's economic history which few would soon forget."

At one point, 20 percent of Minnesota's adult black men and women worked at the New Brighton plant. The meat packers continued to hire black workers, and there were jobs in retail sales, printing, manufacturing and public utilities. Some doors remained closed, however. David Taylor wrote that the Twin Cities breweries generally refused to hire blacks, and so did the major department stores.

For the Mexican Americans, the war brought a change in the pattern of their lives. Many of the young men joined the armed forces. Some of those who remained in St. Paul continued to work in the beet fields, but the trend was toward workers moving away from the fields and into industry. For them, also, new jobs were opening up in defense plants and textile mills, and more jobs were available in the packing plants and on the railroads. Young Mexican women, whose husbands were in service, departed from the old ways and found work in meatpacking and textile plants.

Workers at the Twin Cities Ordnance Plant in Arden Hills.

Steady work and more income helped many families save money for the first time in their lives. Many were able to buy a home. However, when the Mexican American veterans returned home, few of them used G.I. benefits to attend college or learn a trade. They preferred to work in the packing plants or for the railroads, where they could earn more money. Even so, as the 1950s dawned, more Mexican Americans were graduating from high school and attending college. Prosperity made it possible for some families to move off the "flats" and up on the bluffs, following the time-honored example of their predecessors. Within a decade, the "flats" where the Mexican Americans had struggled to adjust to a new life in a new community would disappear forever.

PART V:
A COMMUNITY IN TRANSITION
1950 – 1990

The years after the end of the second World War brought profound changes to St. Paul, as new families formed and deserted a now-crowded city to seek homes beyond it. Ramsey County's historic villages became islands in a sea of suburban sprawl, and the city itself, halted in its development by the depression and by World War II, was faced with aging neighborhoods and a slowly deteriorating downtown.

A trip to the
Minnesota
State Fair meant
dressing up —
and donning one's
newest hat —
in the 1950s.

The 1950s were relatively placid and prosperous years, despite the Korean War and the Cold War struggle with the Soviet Union. But the agents of change were in place. Plans were on the boards for the superhighways that by the 1960s would slice through and partially obliterate once-vibrant neighborhoods, and blueprints were readied for urban renewal programs that would level entire blocks of decaying houses, churches and business or commercial buildings.

The freeway, Interstate 94, severed the state capital complex from downtown St. Paul. More than that, it destroyed neighborhoods that had been home to several generations of newcomers to the city. Kathryn Boardman, writing in the St. Paul Pioneer Press in 1969, described the loss of neighborhoods she called "The Cities Within." North of downtown St. Paul and east of the capitol, she wrote, was a district that once was "European and exciting." Its "houses, duplexes and apartments were packed tight together so that women on one second story porch could talk easily with friends on the one next door."

Modest but deteriorating homes that had clustered about the capitol were torn down in an effort to create a Capitol Approach based on architect Cass Gilbert's original design. Rondo Street, once the heart of the African

The sumptuous Ryan Hotel was one of many St. Paul landmarks razed in the 1960s and 1970s.

Americans' neighborhood, disappeared as I-94 cut through it.

The simple shacks lining Swede Hollow, home for almost 150 years first to French fur traders, then to Swedish, Polish, Italian and Mexican brewery and railroad workers, were burned down. The ravine is now a park. The homes of the Italians and Poles living on the Upper Levee between Chestnut and the High Bridge — a neighborhood that was frequently flooded — were cleared to make way for industrial uses and for Shepard Road. The West Side lowlands — swampy, poorly drained and, again, frequently flooded — also were cleared and Riverview Industrial Park went up.

Downtown in St. Paul's first neighborhood, the rise of the urban renewal movement in the 1960s and 1970s was both a positive and a destructive force. Old St. Paul began to disappear. The buildings that had arisen out of the boom years of the 1880s and gave the city its distinctive character were weeded out as the next great building boom of the 1960s and 1970s got underway.

The majestic Ryan Hotel, built in 1885 at Sixth and Robert streets and St. Paul's social center for years, went down, along with an adjacent block. Although both blocks remained empty so long they were referred to as "super hole," they are the site today of Town Square and its indoor Town Square Park. At Seven Corners, block after block was cleared to build the Civic Center. More blocks were leveled to build Capital Centre, with Osborn Plaza, at Fifth and Wabasha.

Lost in the clearance were buildings that were among the last links with the city's sturdy, bustling past. More importantly, lost also as a result of just two projects — Highway 94 and the Capitol Approach — were more than 15,000 people who lived there and had to be relocated. Many of them were the city's more recent immigrants who were struggling to establish themselves in low-cost housing. With the residents went small business owners, the glove-menders, hat-blockers, tailors and other operators of small service shops located in the old, low-rent buildings.

Even while much was destroyed, much also was saved. The Lower-town National Historic District includes blocks of nineteenth century warehouses and mercantile buildings. They surround Mears Park, known for much of its history as Smith Park, which was named for an early land speculator from Illinois who never lived in St. Paul. The park was renamed in honor of businessman Norman B. Mears, who launched an early effort at preservation of the district. The once-elegant Irvine Park residential district around Governor Ramsey's home at Walnut and Exchange was spared demolition. Some of its homes were among the last remaining pre-Civil War houses in St. Paul. They were restored, and the city's first National Historic District created in 1973.

The preservation and restoration of the Old Federal Courts Building as Landmark Center was a project begun in 1969. Its success helped stem the tear-it-down frenzy of the 1960s and demonstrated to the community and the country that old buildings can be adapted successfully for new purposes. The majestic, turn-of-the-century Richardsonian-Romanesque structure is today "a civic home for the creative energies of the people of this county," in the words of Frank Marzitelli, who played a leading role in its preservation as an arts and cultural center.

A private and public partnership was forged between the Board of Ramsey County Commissioners, who owned Landmark Center and agreed to pay for its maintenance, and Minnesota Landmarks, Inc., a private non-profit organization that agreed to raise the millions of dollars needed to restore it. A compelling issue behind the project was the fact that the city's cultural agencies already had outgrown the St. Paul Arts and Science Center, which was opened in 1964 to house them.

While the community's arts organizations had flowered in the warmth of post-World War II prosperity, the roots of at least two of them — the Schubert Club and the St. Paul Chamber Orchestra — lay in late nineteenth and early twentieth century St. Paul. The Schubert Club, Minnesota's oldest musical organization, grew out of a St. Paul musical tradition that extended as far back as the 1850s and 1860s. Then, music-lovers gathered in each other's homes to play and discuss music. They owned pianos and melodeons that were shipped up the river by steamboats or hauled in by cart. By the 1860s, pianos were being manufactured in St. Paul.

Charles W. W. Borup and his wife held musicals in the 1850s in their elegant villa at Tenth and Wacouta in Lowertown. Borup played the violin while members of his family accompanied him on two grand pianos. Through the years, informal gatherings such as these evolved into the Ladies Musicale. Members met in their homes in the afternoon to do fancy

Charles W. W. Borup, banker and fur trader.

Schubert Club members have contributed generations of talent to the community. This performance was during the 1949-50 season.

work and listen to musical performances by their talented friends. By 1883, the meetings were more formally organized, and in 1888, its name was changed to the Schubert Club, in honor of the Austrian composer.

Emil Oberhoffer, a German-born violinist, pianist and conductor who was stranded in St. Paul in the early 1890s, was hired by the Schubert Club to direct its Ladies' Chorus and newly-formed orchestra. In 1903, when the Minneapolis (now Minnesota) Symphony Orchestra was founded, he became its first conductor.

The Schubert Club held recitals and lectures in a hall on Third Street, but later moved its performances to the St. Paul auditorium and the People's Church. In 1968, the club passed from an all-volunteer organization conducting its business in members' homes to professional management under an executive director. Today, its annual music competition offers one of the most respected venues for recognizing young musicians in the Midwest.

No group, however, was more responsible for the development of music in St. Paul than the German community. The German Singing Society was formed in 1853. It was followed by the formation of the Liederkranz Society and the Beethoven Society. German-born Philip Rohr introduced opera to St. Paul in the early 1860s.

The St. Paul Music Society was a small orchestra that emerged from a group of string players, and its president, George Siebert, presided over the beginnings of orchestral music in St. Paul. During the last half of the nineteenth century, the orchestra under Siebert was the major musical group in Minnesota. Siebert persuaded his brother-in-law, Frank Danz, Sr., to establish the Great Western Band, later the Danz Orchestra and the real roots of the Minneapolis Symphony.

The St. Paul Philharmonic Orchestra, a descendant of several groups of professional musicians who banded together, was America's first fulltime professional chamber orchestra. It was founded by twenty-five professional musicians, with Leonard Sipe, a member of Hamline University's faculty, as the conductor. Under the guidance of Sipe, general manager Stephen Sell, and Dennis Russell Davies, who succeeded Sipe in 1972, the renowned St. Paul Chamber Orchestra was created. In 1980, Davies, in turn, was succeeded by the internationally famous violinist, Pinchas Zuckerman, a conductor of ten years' experience.

St. Paul native Paul Manship's work was displayed at the St. Paul Institute of Arts and Sciences in 1967.

The visual arts also have had a long history in St. Paul. Since the nineteenth century, the Twin Cities area has attracted artists: George Catlin, famed Western painter; Seth Eastman, Fort Snelling commandant and one of the great painters of the Mississippi valley and of Native American life in Minnesota; and S. Holmes Andrews, among the first to paint St. Paul from Cherokee Heights. Representative of that tradition, the St. Paul Gallery and School of Art was founded in 1927 by a group of artists and students. Today it has become the Minnesota Museum of Art.

Newer community cultural groups blossomed in the 1960s and 1970s: COMPAS, a community outreach program for the arts and sciences; the Ramsey County Historical Society, founded in 1949, with its Gibbs Farm Museum, publishing program and series of exhibits in Landmark Center; and United Arts, an outgrowth of two earlier organizations: the St. Paul Institute of Arts and Sciences, created in 1908, and the St. Paul-Ramsey Council of Arts and Sciences, incorporated in 1954 to support the city's cultural organizations.

Candle dipping is just one of the crafts demonstrated at the Ramsey County Historical Society's Gibbs Farm Museum.

The Science Museum of Minnesota is, in a sense, another descendant of the Institute. The museum traces its origins to 1870 when the St. Paul Academy of Natural Sciences was created by a group of St. Paul physicians, scientists and teachers. The group was led by Robert O. Sweeny, a pharmacist and artist. Sweeny designed the state's first great seal, created a series of charming sketches of early St. Paul, and served as Minnesota's first game and fish director. In 1907, the Academy closed, but its

collections were turned over to the Institute. The Institute drew together under one leadership all of the city's musical, educational and literary programs. Based on the concept of a people's university, its programs, lectures, and evening classes represented an idea that was far ahead of its time.

For twenty years, the Institute operated out of three floors of the city auditorium on West Fourth Street. In 1928 it acquired the massive stone mansion built in 1887 by Colonel John Merriam (father of Minnesota's eleventh governor) on the hill behind the present capitol. After another move, in 1964, into the Arts and Science Center, the Science Museum opened its new building at Tenth and Wabasha in 1978. The museum's centerpiece is the spectacular Omnitheater, with its domed seventy-six-foot screen and 70-mm Omnimax projector.

The Minnesota Historical Society, now completing a multi-million dollar history center on a ridge overlooking downtown St. Paul, is in a very real sense the state's "memory" and the keeper of its records. The oldest institution in Minnesota, it was founded in 1849, the year Minnesota became a territory, by a group of settlers led by Alexander Ramsey, the society's first president.

The Society's new history center will gather together in one place its collection of documents and manuscripts, which it has maintained since 1849; its library; a major museum; and its administration offices. The society also administers a network of historic sites throughout Minnesota. In St. Paul, they include James J. Hill's mansion on Summit Avenue; Ramsey's own house in the Irvine Park National Historic District; and the restored and reconstructed Fort Snelling.

St. Paul's love affair with theater predates the city itself. Its origins lie in amateur productions by the Old Fort Snelling Dramatic Club that was organized by soldiers to while away long winter evenings. Frank M. Whiting, former director of the University Theatre at the University of Minnesota, described theater in early St. Paul in an article in RAMSEY COUNTY HISTORY.

"In the summer of 1857," he wrote, "St. Paul, with a population of 10,000, was supporting three professional theatrical companies, a minstrel show, a circus, a professional tent show and an amateur dramatic society." Variety and burlesque shows flourished in St. Paul during the years before and after the Civil War. An opera house was built in 1867 on the site today of the Radisson Hotel on Kellogg Boulevard. Henry Van Liew erected his "People's Theater" two blocks away. Vaudeville, at such theaters as the Garrick at Sixth and St. Peter streets, succeeded burlesque, then met its own demise at the hands of the moving picture which, in turn, transferred its struggle for existence to the home screen.

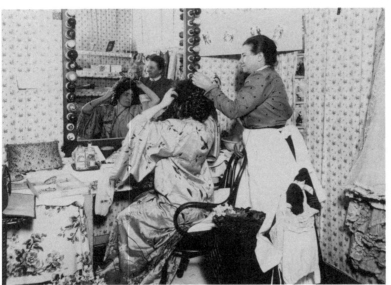

Backstage at the Metropolitan Opera House in St. Paul, Mrs. Leslie Carter prepares for a 1901 performance.

The World Theatre and the now-vacant Orpheum Theater were two of eight movie houses that some seventy years ago formed a downtown theater district extending along Wabasha and St. Peter between Fifth and Tenth streets. The old Capitol Theatre on Seventh Street, between St. Peter and Wabasha, was St. Paul's "million-dollar playhouse." Built within the Hamm Building by William Hamm in 1920, the Capitol was the largest, most expensive, and most elaborate movie palace in the Northwest. It was designed for an opulent era; but, as times began to change, the Capitol became the smaller Paramount, then shrank again into the Norstar — the last (at that time) of the downtown theaters until it closed in 1978.

The late 1970s, however, were years of rich ferment for the city's cultural community. Both the World Theatre and the Capitol came to life again. The World, built in 1910 as the Schubert, gained fame as the home in 1978 of Garrison Keillor's "A Prairie Home Companion" radio show. After a year-long restoration project begun in 1984, the theater reopened in 1985; today it is used by a number of cultural organizations. What remained of the Capitol Theatre also was renovated to house, first, Actors Theater, and now, as Seventh Place Theater, other theater groups. Penumbra Theatre was established in 1977 in the Martin Luther King Center to focus on work that reflects the black experience in America. It was the first public theater in America to present the work of Pulitzer Prize-winning author and playwright August Wilson.

The Great American History Theatre was founded as a COMPAS program in 1978, then incorporated independently in 1981. It produces work with historical themes, including the history of Minnesota. Park Square Theatre was founded in 1975. Film In The Cities, established in 1970 to teach the arts of film-making to junior and senior high school students, now works with professional as well as amateur video artists, writers and composers.

Garrison Keillor, writer/host of "A Prairie Home Companion."

The most spectacular music and theater event for St. Paul in recent years was the building of the Ordway Music Theatre across from Rice Park. It was an enormous effort led by men and women who are descendants of Minnesota's oldest families or linked to the state's major corporations: G. Richard Slade, great-grandson of James J. Hill; Carl B. Drake, Jr., retired board chairman of The St. Paul Companies and descendant of Elias Drake, who built the railroads Hill later on owned; Elizabeth Musser, who helped restore Landmark Center and whose husband was a Weyerhaeuser company executive; and David Lilly, formerly Toro Company's chief executive officer.

The Ordway project was triggered by Sally Ordway Irvine, granddaughter of 3M investor Lucius Pond Ordway. She gave $7 million to the project, then persuaded other family members to join her as contributors. The Ordway opened in January, 1985, as a $46 million glass, copper and mahogany music theater designed and built in the tradition of opera houses, theaters and concert halls in Vienna, Paris and Salzberg. Its opening came at a time when, despite a sharp recession in the early 1980s, the nation still was caught up in the long economic expansion that followed the end of World War II.

Once again, however, not all of St. Paul's people shared in the opportunities ignited by post-World War II prosperity. For many African Americans, the jobs the war years had opened up were sustained, as David Taylor has written in THEY CHOSE MINNESOTA. For those who were veterans, the G. I. bill offered educational advancement. But racial discrimination remained, and it was particularly apparent as St. Paul struggled with the post-war housing shortage. Restrictive covenants in real estate — illegal but still quietly observed — kept black families from buying homes in certain

The downtown Woolworth's was the scene of civil rights demonstrations before blacks were allowed to dine at the lunch counter.

neighborhoods at the same time that urban renewal programs were destroying other neighborhoods where they lived. Home loans and insurance were difficult to arrange, and even federal housing programs discriminated against blacks, Taylor wrote.

Between 1950 and 1970, St. Paul's African American population grew by 388 percent. Much of the growth came during the 1960s, when the struggle for civil rights was sweeping the country. St. Paul wasn't spared the violence of that period. In 1968, rioting broke out over the Labor Day weekend. The rioting was a reflection of similar upheavals that were taking place all over the country. The causes were complex: the civil rights struggle, the assassination of Martin Luther King, the perceived brutality on the part of the police and hostility on the part of government authorities, protests against the Vietnam War, and a pervading sense of hopelessness — all, and perhaps other factors, were underlying causes.

In St. Paul, scores of people were injured in the rioting, and thousands of dollars worth of property was damaged. While the destruction was not as widespread as in many other cities, it spurred the state to draft legislation and the private sector to develop programs to counteract racism. However, the primary beneficiaries have been, in Taylor's words, "a small but cohesive black middle class, leaving the under-educated and unskilled not much more advanced than they were in the 1960s."

St. Paul's Mexican Americans shared in many of the same war-time and post-war opportunities — development of job skills through work in war plants, education for veterans under the G. I. bill, job opportunities for women, and the greater economic stability that increased incomes provided. But they also faced some of the same problems as the African Americans. Young people in the Mexican American community reported that discrimination had tripled over what their parents had faced. The clearance of the West Side "flats" had dislocated families, and in some neighborhoods juvenile deliquency was high, in contrast to the low rates of the 1930s.

Some government agencies and private sector organizations were helping Mexican Americans deal with these problems. In 1968, under the

Mexico's independence from Spain, observed annually on May 5 as Cinco de Mayo, included this patriotic tableau in a 1940 Neighborhood House celebration.

auspices of Neighborhood House, Torre de San Miguel Homes, Inc. offered quality housing to low- and middle-income families. A growing interest in their heritage also has been a strengthening factor for many Mexican Americans and has influenced certain programs. A bilingual-bicultural program for kindergarten through first grade has been offered at West Side schools. In 1974, the governor created the Office of Migrant Affairs, now the Council on Affairs of Spanish Speaking People. A growing number of churches are offering services in Spanish. Some Mexican American families are becoming homeowners and moving away from the West Side. And the business community on Concord Street, in the heart of the community, has been, in recent years, predominantly Mexican American.

Mexican American community leaders emerged during the period following World War II. Nick Castillo, for whom Parque Castillo is named, was a performer, musician, singer and song writer who kept alive the tradition of Mexican folk songs. Frank Rodriquez, a political activist and a state senator from the West Side, was one of the first Mexican Americans to serve in the state legislature. Guadalupe Cruz was a founder of the Our Lady of Guadalupe Society, a women's organization that raised money to help pay off the church mortgage. Maria Rangel Moran founded the Ballet Folklorico Guadalupano to preserve regional Mexican dances. Ramedo Saucedo was director of the Minnesota Historical Society's Mexican American History Project, and served on the society's council.

For the Native Americans, the New Deal programs of the 1930s and the full employment years of World War II brought little prosperity, although more than 2,500 Native American men found work in the fourteen camps set up around the state by the Civilian Conservation Corps (C.C.C.) Indian Division. Thousands of Native Americans also served in the armed forces and more than 400 performed a unique and vital service as "code talkers" — passing information in their own Native American languages, a "code" the enemy could neither identify nor break, since it was almost impossible to counterfeit the sounds. Code talkers were used during both World War I and World War II, almost entirely by the United States marines.

In the years following the war, Minnesota's Indian bands began a major shift in population. Facing discrimination and a scarcity of jobs on their reservations, in other rural areas and in the small towns of the state, they sought work in Minneapolis and St. Paul. The largest settlement, a predominantly Ojibway community, has been around Franklin Avenue in Minneapolis. St. Paul's Indian community has been considerably smaller. Half of its people are Ojibway, and the remaining are Dakota and Winnebago.

The Dakota people are not new to St. Paul. Despite the disruption of their lives created by the 1851 treaties of Traverse des Sioux and Mendota, their history has been continuous in the region. Some Dakota families never left the area. They continued to live near their traditional villages, or on the West Side of St. Paul. Others moved to the Lower and Upper Sioux reservations along the Minnesota River but, disillusioned with the restrictions reservation life placed upon them, moved back to their old homes in Wabasha, Goodhue and Rice counties.

(Left)
Dr. Cornel Pewewardey, principal of the St. Paul Public School's American Indian Magnet school.

(Right)
The Red School House is St. Paul's lone private American Indian school. These children recited a poem for Martin Luther King Day in 1991.

The movement was not without problems. The Dakota could not leave the reservations without special permits — "walking papers" issued by the government. There was division, also, among the Dakota people themselves. Although hunger on the reservations and disgust with unfulfilled governmental promises drove the bands toward the open warfare that erupted in 1862, some of the Dakota either did not participate in the conflict or they actively helped the white settlers.

By 1870, after the expulsion of most of the Dakota people from the state, those who had remained friendly to the whites or who had never left the area in the first place were joined by other groups to form a small but continuing Dakota presence in Minnesota. A few, as David Beaulieu has

On December 26, 1990, several American Indians endured -40° wind chill as they made part of the ninety-mile trip from Fort Snelling to Mankato, in memory of the thirty-eight Dakota hanged in Mankato in 1862.

written in MINNESOTA IN A CENTURY OF CHANGE, remained near Shakopee, where Chief Shakopee had asked Samuel and Gideon Pond to establish a mission and school in 1846. Others lived at Faribault, under the wings of Episcopal Bishop Henry B. Whipple and the French fur trader, Alexander Faribault. Still others lived on Grey Cloud Island in the Mississippi, south of St. Paul, and at Prairie Island in the Mississippi, north of Red Wing.

In 1886, the government purchased land at Prior Lake, Prairie Island, and Wabasha to create a permanent home for the Dakota people. The Prairie Island Sioux, as they are known, are descendants of Mdewakanton bands whose traditional home was around Red Wing. After the 1886 purchase, they settled on Prairie Island. It was the only land in the region that had never been occupied by whites.

The Shakopee band settled on the Prior Lake land, where today they form the Shakopee Mdewakanton Sioux community and operate the thriving Little Six Bingo Palace and Casino. So economically successful has this been that in 1991 the Mdewakanton community awarded a $50,000 grant to Augsburg College in Minneapolis, to be used to create an American Indian Scholarship Fund. The gift, according to Mdewakanton Tribal Chairman Leonard Prescott, is to be matched with other contributions to create a $100,000 endowment fund.

Chief Shakopee, a leader of his people.

Little Six is a beneficiary of the rise of a new activism among the Native Americans that marked the 1960s and affected the lives of American Indians throughout the country. Over the years, federal policy as administered by the bureaucratic and much-maligned Bureau of Indian Affairs had begun to change under pressure from the Native Americans. The National Congress of American Indians (NCAI), founded in 1944, helped engineer a new Indian agenda and create a new sense of activism.

In 1961, the NCAI helped organize the American Indian Chicago Conference. In its sessions at the University of Chicago, the

conference adopted the Declaration of Indian Purpose — still the principal agenda for Native Americans across the country, as Beaulieu noted. Its points emphasized the need to re-establish Indian culture and values; the need to right past wrongs and end current wrongs; the need for access to education and modern resources; and the need for protection against loss.

In 1968, the American Indian Movement (A.I.M.) was formed in Minneapolis. The National Indian Education Association was organized two years later by a group of Minneapolis Indians. They lobbied successfully for passage, in 1972, of the Indian Education Act, designed to support programs for Indian children in public schools throughout the country. Alternative education programs also have been developed. One such program for St. Paul's Indian children is the Red School House, established in the old Irish Catholic parish of St. Vincent's. Indian-sponsored and staffed, the school teaches Indian language and culture, as well as English reading and mathematics, but presented within Indian contexts. The Native American Magnet School in the Mounds Park neighborhood is part of the public school system and represents the St. Paul School District's efforts to improve education for Native Americans.

American Indian Movement members, the Mississippi River Revival, and a number of other groups joined to hold the Two Rivers Cultural Explosion in 1991. Part of the event included a canoe journey from Lake Itasca to Fort Snelling, with periodic monitoring of the Mississippi River's water quality.

Many other organizations have helped. Some of these have been established by the Native Americans themselves: the Upper Midwest Indian Center, the Division of Indian Work of the Minnesota Council of Churches, and the American Indian Opportunities Industrialization Council.

"The Indians have a right to know that their name as a people is not hidden forever from its place among the nations of the earth," Arthur Parker wrote in 1916. In 1989 David Beaulieu wrote eloquently of the threat to the sovereignty of tribal governments by federal and state governments. He cited the "incompetence and irresponsibility of an apathetic federal government."

"Ultimately, the faith of American Indians in the honor of words spoken and agreements made according to the treaty provisions of the U.S. Constitution carried the concept of tribal sovereignty through the federal courts and Congress," he wrote. "In the course of this struggle

the Indians also strengthened, however inadvertently, every American's faith in the Constitution."

It is clear that, with the civil rights struggle of the African Americans and the new activism of the Native Americans, the 1960s and 1970s were a period of social revolution. Significant though those movements were, they were overshadowed by the outburst of anger and protest over the nation's involvement in the war in Southeast Asia. The upheavals of those years affected every person, every man, woman and child, every family, church and school in the United States. However, the tragedy of the war had an immediate and far-reaching effect on St. Paul and Ramsey County. Both city and county opened their doors to a new wave of immigrants, the desperate refugees from the war-torn countries of Southeast Asia — the Hmong, the Vietnamese, the Cambodians and the Laotians.

The bitter heritage of a failed American policy, the Southeast Asians shared a common history. Many had worked for or had supported American civilian and military agencies; or they had fought with American forces in their homelands; or they had been associated with United States-supported governments who had resisted Communist domination of the region. Some had simply opposed the new regimes. With the withdrawal of American troops from the region, the collapse of governments and the realistic fear of reprisals from the Communists who took control in 1975, the flight of the Southeast Asians began.

Some were more fortunate than others. The United States had promised to evacuate those who had worked for the Americans, but in the chaos that accompanied the pull-out of American troops, only a small number escaped. Thousands upon thousands of people were left behind to face deportation or labor camps, the break-up of families, or the murder of family members. Villages were destroyed. Hunger, starvation, perilous and desperate escapes into neighboring countries or across pirate-infested waters were followed by years in refugee camps awaiting resettlement in the United States or elsewhere. It was against this background of terror and loss, with the added harsh and disruptive experience of exile and resettlement, that the first Southeast Asians reached St. Paul in 1976.

In particular danger of

As St. Paul's Southeast Asian population has grown, so has awareness of the newcomers' culture. This Hmong New Year celebration was held at Highland Park High School in 1981.

103

reprisals were the Hmong, from the northern mountains of Laos, who fought with the Clandestine Army organized by the United States' Central Intelligence Agency, and performed dangerous missions. They were the largest group of Southeast Asian refugees to arrive in the United States, and they are by far the largest refugee group in St. Paul and Ramsey County. With those who settled in Minneapolis, as well as St. Paul, the Twin Cities were at one time the largest urban settlement of Hmong in the United States.

The Hmong community has faced an especially difficult struggle to adjust to a highly technical culture that is radically different from their mountain existence in Laos. The Hmong are an ethnic Chinese people who may have originated in Siberia or Mongolia more than 5,000 years ago. They moved into southwestern China and, in the late eighteenth and early nineteenth centuries, migrated to northern Laos. Isolated in their mountains, they grew vegetables and small grains, hunted, and raised livestock. They spoke a language that, until the 1950s, possessed no written alphabet. Formal education was rare; their children were taught orally by their elders.

Tou Xiong reacts to a demand from a dragon in "Hmong Tapestry: Voices from the Cloth," a play written and performed by St. Paul Hmong youth in 1991.

At the beginning of World War II, the Hmong joined the Laotians in fighting invading Japanese forces. In the process, they acquired a reputation as fierce guerrilla fighters. When civil war broke out in 1955, the Hmong allied themselves with the Royal Lao government, then supported by the United States, against the Pathet Lao. It was a conflict that separated Hmong families and forced them out of the hills and into the urbanized lowlands.

When the Pathet Lao took over Laos, reprisals against the Hmong were savage. Thousands fled into Thailand, where they began the long wait for resettlement in the United States.

The first Hmong families reached St. Paul in 1976. Over the next four years, the community expanded rapidly as its leaders sought to reunite separated families. Thus, many were secondary immigrants to Minnesota, arriving from elsewhere in the United States to join families already in St. Paul. The great majority of them settled in the North End and Summit-

University neighborhoods, and on the West Side where, by 1991, they nearly outnumbered the Mexican Americans.

For the Hmong, the extended family is the most important factor in their culture. Hmong families are part of a patrilineal clan system that includes all persons with the same paternal grandparents. They live in households that consist of the eldest male member of the family, his wife, their unmarried children, and their married sons and their families. It is a system that gives the Hmong a sense of belonging and security, but it also generates a willingness to move frequently to remain close to family members.

A lack of language and technical job skills has been a major barrier for the Hmong in their struggle to adapt to their new lives in St. Paul. The Board of Ramsey County Commissioners, the county's welfare office and the City of St. Paul all have been deeply involved in efforts to help not only the Hmong but other Southeast Asian refugees. The refugees themselves have formed such organizations as the Hmong American Partnership and the United Laotian Association. The Lao Family Community, Inc., serves as an information network and organizes educational projects, such as classes in English. Although the Hmong religion is traditionally animistic, many Hmong were converted to Christianity in Laos, and a Hmong Catholic Community, served by a Hmong-speaking French priest, was established at St. Mary's Church in Lowertown.

Observances of Vietnamese May Day have often featured parades. This group marched down Summit Avenue.

The Vietnamese were the second largest group of Southeast Asians in Minnesota, although they settled in smaller numbers in Ramsey County. Like the Hmong, they also had migrated into Vietnam from China and their long history is marked by constant struggle with the Chinese over border territories. With the Communist take-over of South Vietnam in 1975, the Vietnamese who had supported the old regime and the American forces also began their long flight.

Again, the first group of refugees — civil servants, military personnel, teachers, writers, and others who had worked for the American government — were evacuated and resettled relatively quickly in the United States.

Because they were educated people who knew some English and possessed job skills, their adjustment was easier than for those who followed them. The horrors experienced by the "boat people" who fled in fishing boats, and by those who spent years in the relocation camps, are widely known.

The Vietnamese have settled throughout St. Paul and Ramsey County in families that typically include three generations. A Vietnamese Buddhist Association of Minnesota was formed and the Archdiocese of Minneapolis and St. Paul organized a Vietnamese Catholic Community. The Vietnamese Cultural Association of Minnesota (VICAM) was formed to promote literature and the fine arts. The Vietnamese Alliance, organized in 1975, and the Vietnamese League, which was established the next year, are two self-help groups that have evolved from the community itself.

The adjustment of the Vietnamese to American life and culture has been made easier because of their higher level of education. Vietnamese parents place a high value on education, influenced in all likelihood by the strong tradition of education in their homeland where, up until 1975, school was free and mandatory until the fifth grade.

The Cambodians, the third largest Southeast Asian refugee group to settle in Minnesota, fled from one of the most brutal of the Communist regimes in that region. Caught in the struggle against Communist domination of Southeast Asia, the people of Cambodia, now called Kampuchea, saw the government of General Lon Nol overthrown in 1975. Lon Nol had been supported by the United States, and with his downfall, the Cambodian Communists, organized as the Khmer Rouge, installed Pol Pot as leader.

A merciless zealot, Pol Pot evacuated all major cities, forcing his people to work the land. Opponents of his regime, including civil servants, teachers, and intellectuals, were detained and often killed. Millions died by torture, murder, execution, starvation or disease.

Cambodian people poured into Thailand where they waited, often for years, in refugee camps hoping to emigrate to the United States, France, Australia, Canada or some other nation. Among those who reached America and then St. Paul, an estimated two-thirds were women with children whose husbands and other male family members were killed in the Khmer Rouge holocaust.

Although most of the Cambodian refugees were rural peasants with little education, they have a rich history that is symbolized by the temples at Angkor Wat. In 1864, the French, attracted by trade routes to the East, negotiated a treaty creating a French protectorate for Cambodia. However, by the early 1950s, the Vietnamese Communists had challenged the French in a move that eventually led to the overthrow of its ancient monarchy and then of Lon Nol.

In Minnesota and St. Paul, the Cambodian Association of Minnesota and Friends, established in 1975, has worked to bring more refugees, still trapped in the camps in Thailand, to the state for resettlement. The Cambodian American Association in Minnesota was formed in 1978 as a cultural organization that also focuses on helping new arrivals in the region.

The Laotian community is the smallest of the Southeast Asian groups in the Twin Cities and few Laotians live in Ramsey County. The Laotians and the Hmong share a common homeland and heritage, with the Laotians living in the lowland region of Laos and the Hmong in the mountains to the north. The Laotians who fled their country when the Americans withdrew had been allied with the former Laotian government and faced persecution at the hands of the new Communist regime, including seizure of their lands or businesses.

Americanization efforts, with an emphasis on skills needed in today's St. Paul, are continued through agencies such as Lao Family Community. This is the agency's first "graduating class."

The early Laotian arrivals in St. Paul brought with them skills that could be transferred to America's more technical society. Later arrivals from rural areas have had more difficulty in adjusting.

For Laotians, as with other refugees from Southeast Asia, the family is the central social unit. Great effort is made to maintain Laotion customs within the family. Large extended families sometimes include four generations living together in one household. The Laotion community, however, includes many single men who had to leave their families behind when they fled their country.

As the 1980s ended, the new willingness on the part of the Soviet Union to permit emigration produced a flood of Soviet Jews into St. Paul where the Jewish Family Service resettled 300 in four years. In 1991, about 800 more families from Russia will be resettled in the Twin Cities area. However, Southeast Asians made up 95 percent of the refugees who settled in St. Paul's East Metro area during the 1980s. Many of them have felt much of the same prejudice and discrimination experienced by the many other ethnic and nationality groups who over the years have found new homes in the region. Settling in older neighborhoods where other minority groups share the same need for low-cost housing, the Southeast Asians sometimes seem to threaten the security of the earlier and more established

The International Institute, through its Festival of Nations, outreach efforts and other activities, has done much to promote multi-cultural understanding in St. Paul. This picture is from the 1949 Festival of Nations.

groups, but this is a familiar pattern seen over and over again in St. Paul, as one new immigrant or refugee group after another arrived to settle in the midst of the older, established communities. Tensions and rumors inevitably seem to have arisen — many of them rooted in the elementary fear of competition for jobs; others stemming from customs that appear to be strange; from religious differences; from a lack of knowledge about the newcomers; and from language barriers that shut off communication. As it always has, acceptance will come, but it will take time and effort from the newcomers and the more established community.

It may very well be the children who will lead them. Through the years, St. Paul's schools have been in the forefront of the effort to help newcomers adapt to American ways, and the schools often have been a child's first point of contact with a new and often bewildering life. Teachers — some of them graduates of a teacher-training program operated out of the top floor of the old Central High School in downtown St. Paul — have taught English to generations of immigrant children in the nineteenth century and the early twentieth century when the emphasis was on the melting-pot concept of Americanization. Today, as the twentieth century is nearing its end, English is taught as a second language and there is a new realization of the value of preserving the strengths of other cultures.

New skills and different skills are part of the arsenal teachers draw upon today in the classrooms of the city and the county, including the ability to use computers. So is the knowledge of a second language. This is an asset that is not new to Minnesota schools. In many Norwegian settlements of Minnesota, teachers were required to speak Norwegian in order to communicate with their youngest pupils. German was taught as a second language in the St. Paul schools before World War I.

Inherent in many immigrants to St. Paul through the years has been a longing for the homeland and the lingering hope that one day they might return home. Some have, but for the refugees from Southeast Asia, this is an option that might well remain closed. In many ways, the Southeast Asian immigrants have come the farthest — in terms of distance, language and cultural heritage. As did the immigrants and refugees who preceded them, they have helped to enrich the cultural diversity that is St. Paul's legacy, by adding their native customs and festivals to those of other ethnic and national groups who have long been a part of the fabric of the city's life.

ST. PAUL NEAR THE END OF A CENTURY AND BEYOND ...

The history of St. Paul is the story of the people who have arrived here and those who were here to meet them. The history is a tapestry of peoples, a tapestry with a pattern that continually changes. Even as this history is being written, new people continue to arrive from Southeast Asia, from the Soviet Union, from Africa, from many Spanish-speaking countries and from other places. Projections indicate that by the end of this century, more than 50 percent of the children enrolled in St. Paul's public schools will be children of color. This figure alone says much about what is going on in the community today, and about who will live here in the first quarter of the twenty-first century.

As late-twentieth-century cultural diversification of St. Paul proceeds, the community once again is searching for a new vision of the political, social and economic aspects of community living and new community-wide plans of action. This look at the past is a reminder that both the nation and the community of St. Paul have sought and found new, common visions of community and plans of action in the past. History also is a reminder that the forging of each solution has taken time, and was neither perfect nor permanent. As St. Paul celebrates its 150th year, and as a new century dawns for the nation, the hope remains that the community can and will draw from the experiences of its past to create a community that encompasses as many as possible. This is perhaps the major lesson of the first 150 years, as those who will share in the future face it together.

READ MORE ABOUT ST. PAUL'S HISTORY

Information for **SAINT PAUL — THE FIRST 150 YEARS** and a related school curriculum was drawn from more than 150 sources. The researcher and the author wish to thank the Minnesota Historical Society, Ramsey County Historical Society, University of Minnesota Wilson Library, St. Paul Public Library, James J. Hill Reference Library, Ramsey County Library (Roseville branch) and Archdiocese of Minneapolis-St. Paul Archives for use of materials and assistance rendered.

Perhaps the definitive reference work available on Minnesota's ethnic groups is THEY CHOSE MINNESOTA, a book published in 1981 by the Minnesota Historical Society. This book, which was the result of an eight-year Minnesota Ethnic History Project, details the history of about sixty ethnic groups in the state. Its excellent index and detailed footnotes provide easy access to materials about ethnic groups in St. Paul, as well as further sources of information. It is hoped that THEY CHOSE MINNESOTA will be updated as the years go by, and as ethnic groups continue to make an impact upon the state.

For the sake of brevity, readers are directed to the footnotes in THEY CHOSE MINNESOTA for materials on specific ethnic groups. One resource drawn upon by THEY CHOSE MINNESOTA is the Immigration History and Research Center at the University of Minnesota which maintains information on immigrants from 1890 onward. It, too, must be cited as one of the key resources for those interested in immigration history in St. Paul and the state.

Other useful information about St. Paul history may be found in the pages of several publications. The articles published in RAMSEY COUNTY HISTORY, the Ramsey County Historical Society's magazine, are sources of information on the city's ethnic groups, neighborhoods, institutions and people. Other articles specific to St. Paul may also be found in MINNESOTA HISTORY, the quarterly magazine of the Minnesota Historical Society; ACTA ET DICTA (published by the Catholic Historical Society from 1907 until 1936); GOPHER HISTORIAN (an earlier MHS history magazine published for Minnesota youth); and ROOTS (the MHS publication that succeeded GOPHER HISTORIAN.)

The many newspapers published during St. Paul's history are also an important resource. Microfiche reels of back issues of daily newspapers are available for viewing at MHS, the downtown St. Paul Public Library, the Roseville branch of the Ramsey County Library, and the University of Minnesota's Wilson Library. The MHS newspaper room includes copies of the many world language and neighborhood newspapers that have flourished here for more than 100 years. Newspapers of some of the city's secondary schools have also been preserved here.

When using newspapers, be aware that available indexes at city and county libraries only date back about twenty years. For earlier articles, check the ST. PAUL HISTORY AND BUSINESS INDEX at the downtown St. Paul Public Library. This very useful index is a listing of a collection of articles dating back more than 100 years.

Other resources drawn upon include St. Paul and Ramsey County maps from the county and state historical societies, public and private agency studies, early St. Paul census records and city directories dating back to 1854. Many of the city's churches and organizations, including many with ethnic roots, have also published histories, which can be found at state, city and county libraries.

One final source used was that of written research papers and master's theses, many of which are on file at the Minnesota Historical Society.

Major sources used in researching **SAINT PAUL — THE FIRST 150 YEARS** include:

A History of the City of St. Paul, St. Paul: Minnesota Historical Society, 1876.

Andrews, General C.C., editor. *History of St. Paul, Minnesota.* Syracuse, NY: D. Mason and Co., 1890.

Baker, James H., Hubbard, Lucius F., Murray, William P., Upham, Warren, editors. *Minnesota in Three Centuries, 1655-1908.* St. Paul: Minnesota Historical Society, 1908.

Blegen, Theodore C. *Minnesota: A History of the State.* Minneapolis: University of Minnesota Press, 1963. (An edition of this book with an additional chapter by Russell Fridley was published in 1975.)

Board of Commissioners. *Minnesota in the Civil and Indian Wars, 1861-65.* St. Paul: Pioneer Press Co., 1899.

Brink, Carol. *The Twin Cities.* New York: McMillan Company, 1961.

Castle, Henry. *History of St. Paul and Vicinity: A Chronicle of Progress and Narrative Account of the Industries, Institutions and People of the City and its Tributory Territory.* Chicago and New York: Lewis Publishing Company, 1912.

Christiansen, Theodore. *History of the State and Its People.* Chicago: American Historical Society, Inc., 1935.

Clark, Clifford E., Jr., editor. *Minnesota in a Century of Change.* St. Paul: Minnesota Historical Society, 1989.

Corrigan, Joseph. *History of St. Mark's and the Midway District.* Self-published, 1939.

Dahl, June Wilkinson. *Footprints: A History of the American Red Cross.* St. Paul Area Chapter, American Red Cross, 1981.

Ebbott, Elizabeth for the League of Women Voters of Minnesota. Rosenblatt, Judith, ed. *Indians in Minnesota* (Fourth Edition). Minneapolis: University of Minnesota Press, 1985.

Edwards, Maurice Dwight, D.D. *History of the Synod of Minnesota Presbyterian Church, United States of America.* USA: Synod of Minnesota Presbyterian Church, 1927.

Empson, Donald. *On the Street Where You Live.* St. Paul: Witsend Press, 1974.

Fairbanks, Evelyn. *The Days of Rondo.* St. Paul: Minnesota Historical Society Press, 1990.

Flanagan, John T. *Theodore Hamm in Minnesota: His Family and Brewery.* Minneapolis: Pogo Press, 1989.

Folwell, William Watts. *A History of Minnesota.* St. Paul: Minnesota Historical Society, 1921-30, Vols. I-IV.

Foster, Mary Dillon. *Who's Who Among Minnesota Women.* M.D. Foster, 1924.

Gilman, Rhoda. *Northern Lights: The Story of Minnesota's Past.* St. Paul: Minnesota Historical Society, 1989.

Glewwe, Lois, ed. *South St. Paul Centennial*. Topeka, Kansas: Josten's, Inc., 1987.

Granger, Susan W., Murphy, Patricia. *Historic Sites Survey of St. Paul and Ramsey County, 1980-83: Final Report*. St. Paul: Ramsey County Historical Society and the St. Paul Heritage Preservation Commission, 1983.

Hansen, Eric C. *The Cathedral of St. Paul: An Architectural Biography*. St. Paul: Cathedral of St. Paul, 1990.

Heilbron, Bertha L. *The Thirty-Second State; A Pictorial History of Minnesota*. St. Paul: The Minnesota Historical Society, 1958. (A second edition of this book was published in 1966.)

Hennessy, W.B. *Past and Present of St. Paul, Minnesota*. Chicago: S. J. Clarke Publishing Co., 1906.

Hiebert, Gareth (pen name Oliver Towne). *St. Paul is My Beat*. St. Paul: North Central Publishing Co., 1958.

Heibert, Gareth (pen name Oliver Towne). *Once Upon A Towne*. St. Paul: North Central Publishing Co., 1959.

History of the Police and Fire Departments of the Twin Cities: Their Origins in Early Village Days and Progress to 1900. Minneapolis/St. Paul: American Land and Title Register Association, 1899.

Hoag, Robert. *Churches of St. Paul: A Directory*. Self-published, 1976.

Hoag, Robert. *The Hotels of St. Paul*. Self-published, 1975.

Hoag, Robert. *Hotels in St. Paul: A Directory of Proprietors and Managers*. Self-published, 1972.

Hoag, Robert. *St. Paul Theatres, Halls, Etc*. Self-published, 1975.

Hobart, Chauncey. *History of Methodism in Minnesota*. Red Wing: Red Wing Printing Co., 1887.

Hoffman, William. *Those Were the Days*. Minneapolis: T. S. Denison and Co., 1961.

Hoffman, William. *West Side Story II*. Minneapolis: T. S. Denison and Co., 1961.

Holbrook, Franklin F. *St. Paul and Ramsey County in the War of 1917-1918*. St. Paul: Ramsey County War Records Commission, 1929.

Josephy, Alvin M., Jr. *The Indian Heritage of America*. Boston: Houghton Mifflin Company, 1991.

Kennon, Peggy Korsmo. *Discover St. Paul: A Short History of Seven St. Paul Neighborhoods*. St. Paul: Ramsey County Historical Society, 1979.

Kunz, Virginia Brainard. *The Mississippi and St. Paul*. St. Paul: Ramsey County Historical Society, 1987.

Kunz, Virginia Brainard. *From Muskets to Missiles: A Military History of Minnesota*. St. Paul: Minnesota Statehood Centennial Commission, 1958.

Kunz, Virginia Brainard. *St. Paul: Saga of an American City*. Woodland Hills, Calif.: Windsor Publications, Inc., 1977.

Kunz, Virginia Brainard. *St. Paul: A Modern Renaissance.* Northridge, Calif.: Windsor Publications, Inc., 1986.

Martin, Albro. *James J. Hill and the Opening of the Northwest.* New York: Oxford University Press, 1976. (This book was reprinted by the Minnesota Historical Society in 1991.)

Martin, Calvin, Ed. *The American Indian and the Problem of History.* New York and Oxford: Oxford University Press, 1987.

McClure, Ethel. *More Than a Roof: The Development of Minnesota Poor Farms and Homes for the Aged.* St. Paul: Minnesota Historical Society, 1968.

Neill, Edward D. *History of the Minnesota Valley.* Minneapolis: North Star Publishing Company, 1882. (This book includes accounts by other authors, including a history of the Dakota Conflict by Charles S. Bryant.)

Neill, Edward D. *History of Ramsey County and the City of St. Paul.* Minneapolis: North Star Publishing Company, 1881.

Newson, T. M. *Pen Pictures of St. Paul.* St. Paul: Self-published, 1886.

One Hundred Years in the St. Paul Pioneer Press. St. Paul: St. Paul Pioneer Press, 1949.

Plaut, W. Gunther. *The Jews in Minnesota: The First 75 Years.* New York: American Jewish Historical Society, 1959.

Poatgieter, A. Hermina and Dunn, James Taylor, editors. *Gopher Reader: Minnesota's Story in Words and Pictures. Selections from the Gopher Historian.* St. Paul: Minnesota Historical Society and Minnesota Statehood Centennial Commission, 1958.

Pyle, Joseph Gilpin. *The Life of James J. Hill.* Garden City, New York: Doubleday, Page and Co., 1917.

Reardon, James. *The Catholic Church in the Diocese of St. Paul.* St. Paul: The North Central Publishing Co., 1952.

St. Paul Public Schools. *A Collection of Memories: Teacher Memories from 1910-60.* St. Paul: St. Paul Public Schools, 1970.

Schmid, C. F. *Social Saga of Two Cities — An Ecological and Statistical Study of Minneapolis and St. Paul Social Trends.* Minneapolis Council of Social Agencies, 1937.

Sickels, Alice L. *Around the World in St. Paul.* Minneapolis: University of Minnesota Press, 1945.

Spangler, Earl. *The Negro in Minnesota.* Minneapolis: T. S. Denison and Co., 1963.

Vogt, James. *Desnoyer Park.* St. Paul: Desnoyer Park Improvement Association, 1990.

West, Nathaniel. *The Ancestry, Life and Times of Hon. Henry Hastings Sibley, L.L.D.* St. Paul: Pioneer Press Publishing Co., 1889.

Williams, J. Fletcher. *A History of the City of St. Paul.* St. Paul: Minnesota Historical Society. First published by the Minnesota Historical Society in 1876, this book was reissued in 1983 by MHS and is still available for purchase.

Williams, J. Fletcher. *History of Ramsey County and the City of St. Paul.* Minneapolis: The North Star Publishing Company, 1881.

INDEX

A

Acker, William H., 37
Actors Theater, 96
Adams, John Quincy, 75
African Americans, 9, 21, 43, 56, 74-78, 82, 84, 85, 88, 90, 97, 98, 103
Alcoholism, 28, 72
American Fur Company, 11, 16, 20, 23
American Indian Chicago Conference, 101
American Indian Movement (A.I.M.), 102
American Jewish World, 55
Americanization classes, 70
Ancker Hospital, 45, 71
Andrews, S. Holmes, 94
Anti-German hostility, 58
Anti-lynching bill, 71, 77
Antitrust lawsuit, 67
Anti-war demonstrations, 59
Appeal, The, 55, 75
Armstrong, Emma Elizabeth, 72
Associated Charities of St. Paul, 63
Assumption Church, 15, 25, 31, 59
Assumption School, 29, 49
Atheneum, 32, 51
Austrian-Hungarians, 51

B

B'ai Brith, 49
B'nai Zion synagogue, 49
Backus, Carrie Haskins, 71
Baird, Julian, 85
Baker, Robert Orr, 60
Baldwin School, 29, 48
Ballet Folklorico Guadalupano, 99
Baptist Hill, 49
Barker-Karpis gang, 81
Battle of Bull Run, 37
Battle of Gettysburg, 37, 38
Battle of Kaposia, 16, 22
Battle of Murfreesboro, 39
Battle of Shiloh, 39
Battle of Tupelo, 37
Battle of Wood Lake, 42
Beaulieu, David, 100, 102
Beaulieu, Elizabeth, 21
Beethoven Society, 93
Benevolent Society of Erin, 33
Bermeier, Clara Linz, 71
Best, Joel E., 62

Bishop, Harriet, 21, 28, 29, 56, 61
Bivens, Angelina, 30
Blegen, Theodore C., 46, 47
Board of Ramsey County Commissioners, 92, 105
Boeckmann, Dr. Egil, 69
Bohemian Gymnastics Association Sokol, 60
Bootlegging, 79, 80
Borup, Charles W. W., 21, 92
Bottineau, Pierre and Charles, 18
Bramhall, Florence Elfelt, 72
Bremer, Edward, 80
Bremer, Otto, 80
Brissett, Edmund, 13, 20
Brothels, 62
Brown, Joseph R., 23
Brunson, Reverend, Alfred, 8, 9
Burial mounds, 52
Burlington Railroad, 67

C

Cambodian American Association in Minnesota, 107
Cambodian Association of Minnesota and Friends, 107
Camp Cold Water, 7, 10, 11
Campbell, Colin, 21
Campbell, Scott, 21
Capital Centre, 91
Capitol Approach, 90, 91
Capitol Theatre, 96
Carver's Cave, 5, 15
Carver, Jonathan, 4, 5
Castillo, Nick, 99
Castle, Henry A., 58
Catholic Temperance Society of St. Paul, 33
Catholic Total Abstinence Union of America, 72
Central High School, 108
Central House, 28
Chapel of St. Paul, 17
Charles, Mrs. Henrietta, 62
Cherrier, Denis, 16, 20, 21
Chief Cloudman, 8
Chief Shakopee, 101
Chief Wabasha, 41
Chinese Education Society, 51
Christ Church, 50
Church of St. Louis, 48

Cinco de Mayo, 83
Civil rights struggle, 98, 103
Civil War, 33, 35-38, 40, 43, 44, 51, 52, 56, 61, 62
Civilian Conservation Corps (C.C.C.) Indian Division, 99
Civilian Conservation Corps (CCC), 86
Cleveland, Horace W. S., 73
Clewett, James R., 16, 17
Clewett, Rose, 17, 29
Clifford, Nina, 63
Code talkers, 99
Community Chest, 63
Community playground movement, 72
Como Park, 73
Como Zoo, 74
COMPAS, 94, 97
Congressional Medal of Honor winner, 37
Connemara Patch, 57
Constitutional convention, 34
Contraband laborers, 43
Cook, Dr. Thomas S., 77
Council of Jewish Women, 71
Council on Affairs of Spanish Speaking People, 99
"Coup d'anee", 5
Cretin, Bishop Joseph, 19, 33
Crump, Dr. J. Walton, 77
Cruz, Guadelupe, 99
Czechoslovakian Protective Society, 51

D

Daily Volks Zeitung, 31, 71
Dakota, 2-6, 9, 10, 21-23, 36, 41, 52, 100
Dakota Conflict of 1862, 31, 40-42
Danes, 21, 55
Davies, Dennis Russell, 94
Dayton's Bluff, 5, 8, 12, 17, 40, 48, 52, 53, 57
Depression, 46, 47, 63, 69, 74, 81, 84-87
Der Wanderer, 55
Desnoyer, Stephen, 11
Dillinger, John, 81
Dr. Franklin No. 2, 27
Du Luth, Sieur, 3, 4
Dubuque and St. Paul Packet Company, 33

E

Earl of Selkirk, 7
East Side, 33, 44, 48, 50, 52, 64
East Side Presbyterian Church, 51
Eastern European Catholics, 57
Eastern European Jews, 82
Eastman, Seth, 7, 8, 94
'l Dieciseis di Setiembre, 83

1837 treaties, 10
Emerson, Dr. John, 9
Episcopalians, 50
Evans, William, 12, 21

F

Family Service of St. Paul, 63
Faribault, Alexander, 101
Federal relief program, 85
Fenian Brotherhood, 57
Fifth Minnesota Infantry Regiment, 38
Film In The Cities, 97
First African American physician, 77
First Baptist Church, 49
First birth, 17
First black criminal lawyer, 76
First black legislative representative, 74
First brewery in Minnesota, 32
First capitol, 28
First governor, 35
First hospital in Minnesota, 29, 61
First Lutheran church, 34
First marriage, 16
First Minnesota Infantry Regiment, 37
First National Bank, 31
First newspaper, 30
First Presbyterian church, 48
First Ramsey County Courthouse, 28
First schools, 28
Flandrau, Grace Hodgson, 72
Folwell, W. W., 6
Forbes, William H., 22
Forrestal, Anne Egan, 71
Fort Garry, 7, 24
Fort Ridgely, 41
Fort Snelling, 6-12, 16-18, 20-23, 28, 35, 37, 40, 42, 43, 55, 56
Fountain Cave, 11, 12
Francis, Nellie Griswold, 71
Francis, W. T., 77
Frankel, Esther, 71
Free day nursery, 74
French Canadian voyageurs, 52
Frogtown, 44, 51
Fugitive slaves, 43

G

G.I. benefits, 88
Galtier, Father Lucien, 17, 19, 20
gambling, 79, 81
Gauthier, Julie Celina, 72
German Emigration Society, 31
German Jews, 58, 74
German Lutherans, 50

German Reading Society, 32
German Singing Society, 93
Germania Life Insurance Company, 59
Gervais, Benjamin, 7, 11, 14, 17, 18, 22
Gervais, Pierre, 11, 18
Gibbs Farm Museum, 94
Gleckman, Leon, 80
Gloeser, Laura Dussair, 71
Goodhue, James M., 23, 27, 30
Great Census War of 1890, 65
Great Northern railway strike, 67
Green Lantern, 78
Grey Cloud Island, 101
Guerin, Vetal, 18-20
Guild of Catholic Women, 83
Guise, Mable Hansen, 71

H

Hall Brothers Barber Shop, 76
Hallie Q. Brown Center, 78
Hamm Building, 96
Hamm, Theodore, 31
Hamm, William Jr., 80
Hamm, William Sr., 80, 96
Harriet Island, 73, 74
Hays, John, 12, 15, 16
Hebrew Ladies Benevolent Society, 49
Heckman, A. A., 84, 85
Hennepin, Father Louis, 4
Hennessy, W. B., 20
Hession, Minnie Fay, 71
Hickman, John Henry, 77
Hickman, Robert, 43, 77
Highland Park, 74, 82
Highland Park water tower, 77
Hill, James J., 23, 24, 33, 53, 63, 64, 67, 80, 95, 97
Hill, Louis W., 69, 84
Hinrich, Ferdinand, 52
Hmong community, 104-105
Hoffman, Bill, 64, 65, 87
Hollyhocks, 79
Hollywood Club, 79
Holman Field, 88
Holy Redeemer Catholic Church, 49
Home for the Friendless, 61
Hook and Ladder Company, 45
House for Emigrants, 47
House of Hope Presbyterian Church, 48, 50
House of the Good Shepherd, 61
Howard, Ellen, 71
Howell, Owen, 75, 76
Hungarians, 51
Hurley, Mary Handran, 71

Hutchins, Morgan L., 64
Hutton, Samantha "Long Kate", 62, 63

I

Incorporation as a city in 1854, 28
Incorporation as a town, 28
Indian Education Act, 102
interurban streetcar lines, 53-55, 88
Ireland, Archbishop John, 33, 46, 49, 51, 57, 66
Ireland, Eliza, 71
Ireland, Ellen, 71
Irish-American Colonization Society, 46
Irvine Park National Historic District, 95
Irvine, John R., 26, 29
Irvine, Sally Ordway, 97
Italian immigrants, 52

J

Jackson, Angelina, 29
Jackson, Henry, 22, 26, 30
Jewish immigrants, 52
Jones, Eva, 72

K

Kaposia, 5, 8, 9, 16, 17, 21, 22, 28, 53
Kathio, 3, 4
Keillor, Garrison, 96
Kelly, Margaret Walsh, 72
Kenyon, Sophie Greve, 72
kidnapping, 80, 81
King, Josias, 37
Kittson, Norman W., 23, 30
Kittsondale, 24
Kordosky, Mary Frances, 71

L

LaBissonniere, Isaac, 18
Ladies Musicale, 92
Ladies Relief Association, 61
Lake Phalen, 55
Lambert's Landing, 13
Landmark Center, 28, 67, 92, 94
Laotian community, 107
Larans, Genevieve, 17
Little Crow, 2, 8, 9, 41, 42
Little Six Bingo Palace and Casino, 101
Lower Landing or levee, 13, 14, 22, 38, 43, 44, 56, 72, 74
Lower Payne Avenue neighborhood, 52
Lowertown National Historic District, 92
Lyles, T. H., 76
Lynching, 77

M

Macalester Park, 54
Margolis, Rabbi H. S., 85
Market Street Methodist Church, 49
Marks, Morris and Henry, 32
Martin Luther King Center, 96
Marzitelli, Frank, 92
Mazurka Hall, 51
McClure, Ethel, 61
McDonald, Donald, 11
McGhee, Frederick L., 76
Mc Watt, Arthur C., 75-78, 88, 89
Mdewakanton, 4, 5, 30, 101
Mears Park, 49, 92
Mendota, 3, 10, 11, 16-18, 20, 22, 23, 30, 79
Merriam Park, 44, 54, 66
Merriam, Colonel John, 95
Merrick Community Center, 64
Mexican Americans, 81-83, 98, 99, 105
Meyer, Henry, 31
Minneapolis Symphony Orchestra, 93
Minneapolis Tribune, 65
Minnesota Club, 44, 60
Minnesota Federation of Women's Clubs, 71
Minnesota Historical Society, 20, 32, 42, 95, 99
Minnesota in a Century of Change, 101
Minnesota Museum of Art, 94
Minnesota National Guard, 38, 54, 59
Minnesota Pioneer, 23, 30
Minnesota Public Safety Commission, 59
Minnesota State Fair, 54, 62
Minnesota State Federation of Colored
     Women, 71
Minnesota Supreme Court, 77
Minnesota Territory, 26, 27
Mitchell, Colonel Alexander M., 27
Mitchell, William, 85
Moffett's Castle, 28
Moran, Maria Rangel, 99
Morin, Francois, 18
Moss, Henry L., 28
Mounds Park, 52
Mount Carmel Societies of Women, 50
Mount Zion Hebrew Congregation, 32
Mount Zion Temple, 49, 64
Muench, Adolph, 52
Murray, William Pitt, 80

N

National Association for the Advancement
     of Colored People (NAACP), 77
National Association of Patriotic Instructors, 60
National Congress of American Indians
     (NCAI), 101

National German-American Bank, 48
National Indian Education Association, 102
Native Americans, 4, 21, 22, 99-103
Native American Magnet School, 102
Neighborhood House, 64, 65, 82
Neill, Reverend Edward Duffield, 29, 37, 48
New Brighton, 54
New England Yankees, 10
Newman, Cecil, 88
Newport, Eliza Thompson Edgerton, 72
North End, 51
Northern Belle, 37
Northern Securities Company, 67
Northerner, 43
Norwegian settlements, 108

O

O'Connor system, 79, 80
Oakland Cemetery, 51, 62
Oberhoffer, Emil, 93
Obst, Elsa Redeker, 71
Odone, Father Nicholas, 50
Ohio Life Insurance and Trust Company, 34
Ojibway, 2-4, 6, 21, 22, 25, 100
Old Federal Courts Building, 67
Old Fort Snelling Dramatic Club, 23
Old-stock North Americans, 26
Ordway Music Theatre, 97
Orpheum Theater, 96
Our Lady of Guadalupe Church, 82, 83
Our Lady of Guadelupe Society, 99

P

Panic of 1857, 44
Park Square Theatre, 97
Penumbra Theatre, 96
People's Church, 93
Perry, Abraham, 7, 11, 17
Perry, Adele, 20
Perry, Mary Ann, 20, 29
Perry, Rose, 17
Phalen Creek, 4, 5, 23, 34, 52, 57
Phalen Park, 73
Phelan, Edward, 12, 15, 16, 21
Pierre "Pig's Eye" Parrant, 11-14
Pike, Lieutenant Zebulon, 1, 2, 5, 13
Pilgrim Baptist Church, 43
Pioneer Guard, 36
Polish Jews, 49
Pond, Reverend J. W., 17
Pond, Samuel and Gideon, 8
post office and federal building, 47
Prairie du Chien, 5, 9
Prairie Island Sioux, 101

Prescott, Leonard, 101
Presley, Bartlett, 31
Prince, Mayor John, 38, 44
prohibition, 70, 72, 78, 80
prostitution, 79, 81
Protestant Home of St. Paul, 61
Protestant missions, 17
public baths, 73
public drinking fountains, 70
public welfare, 84
Pullman Porter Brotherhood, 78

R

Railroad Immigration House, 47
Railroad Island, 52
Ramsey County History, 60, 62, 75, 95
Ramsey County League of Women Voters, 71
Ramsey County Nursing Home, 62
Ramsey County Poor Farm, 54, 61-62
Ramsey County WCTU, 72
Ramsey Hill neighborhood, 53
Ramsey, Alexander, 26-27, 36, 41, 48, 56, 95
rationing, 60, 88
Ravoux, Father Augustine, 19
Red River ox carts, 25
Red River Transportation Company, 24
Red School House, 102
Regan, Ann, 79
relief efforts, 84, 85
Republican Women's Club, 71
restrictive covenants, 97
Rice Park, 23, 47, 72, 73, 97
Rice, Henry M., 26, 35, 53, 63
Riverview Industrial Park, 91
Robert, Captain Louis, 29, 80
Robinson, Mary E., 63
Rodriquez, Frank, 99
Rolette, Joe, 34
Romanian Orthodox Church, 51
Rondo Street, 49, 75, 78, 90
Rose, Benjamin, 32
Roseville, 54
Rump Territory of Wisconsin, 26
Rumsey, Matilda, 29
runaway girls, 71
Russian Jews, 49
Ryan Hotel, 91

S

sabotage, 87
Sacred Thirst Total Abstinence Society, 72
Saint Paul House, 28, 31
Sanborn, John B., 37
Sanborn, Mrs. John B., 61

Santee, or eastern, Dakota, 5
Saucedo, Ramedo, 99
Schoonmaker, Harriet Warner, 71
Schroeder, Henry, 54
Schubert Club, 92, 93
Science Museum of Minnesota, 94
Scott, Dred, 9
Selby Avenue tunnel, 53
Selby, Mrs. Jeremiah, 29
Selkirk colony, 7, 11, 21
Sell, Stephen, 94
Shakopee Mdewakanton Sioux, 101
Sherman, Marshall, 37
Shields Guards, 33
Sibley, Henry Hastings, 20-23, 26, 35, 42
Siebert, George, 93
Sipe, Leonard, 94
Sisters of St. Joseph, 20, 61, 71
slackers, 59
Slater, Katherine Louise Dunn, 71
slot machines, 81
Smith Park, 72, 92
Smith, Leona O., 77
Snelling, Colonel Josiah, 7
Society for the Relief of the Poor, 63, 64
Sons of Abraham, 48
Sons of Jacob, 48
Sons of Zion, 48
Southeast Asians, 102-107
Soviet Jews, 107
Spanish influenza, 69
Spanish-American War, 54
speakeasies, 78
St. Agatha's Conservatory, 71
St. Agnes Church, 31, 48
St. Ambrose Church, 49
St. Anthony Park, 44, 54
St. Antonio de Padua Benefit Society, 50
St. James African Methodist Church, 48
St. John's Hospital in St. Paul, 77
St. Joseph's Academy, 20, 71
St. Joseph's Hospital, 29, 60
St. Mark's Episcopal Church, 43
St. Mary's Church, 48
St. Mary's Romanian Orthodox Church, 51
St. Michael's Church, 48
St. Patrick's Day parades, 33
St. Paul Academy of Natural Sciences, 94
St. Paul and Pacific Railroad, 24, 44
St. Paul Arts and Science Center, 92
St. Paul Association of Commerce, 84
St. Paul auditorium, 93
St. Paul bridge, 44
St. Paul Cathedral, 19, 20, 24, 30, 33, 37, 49, 66

St. Paul Chamber Orchestra, 92, 94
St. Paul City Hall-Ramsey County
    Courthouse, 28, 46, 76, 84, 85
St. Paul Echo, 75
St. Paul Gallery and School of Art, 94
St. Paul Institute of Arts and Sciences, 94
St. Paul Music Society, 93
St. Paul Negro Business League, 78
St. Paul Parks, Playgrounds and Public
    Buildings Department, 77
St. Paul Philharmonic Orchestra, 94
St. Paul Pioneer and Democrat, 39
St. Paul Pioneer Press, 55, 60, 79, 90
St. Paul Press, 38
St. Paul Recorder, 88
St. Paul Street Railway Company, 53
St. Paul Union Depot, 44, 47, 57, 66
St. Paul Urban League, 78, 86
St. Paul Volunteer Aid Society, 39
St. Paul Volunteers, 37
St. Paul-Ramsey Council of Arts and
    Sciences, 94
St. Peter Claver Catholic Church, 48
St. Stanislaus Catholic Church, 48
Stevens, Reverend Jedediah, 8
Stewart, Dr. J. H., 37
Stock market crash, 80, 84
Stokes, Mrs. M. L., 30
streetcar strike, 68
Summit Avenue, 15, 48, 52, 68, 94
Summit-University neighborhoods, 74, 104
Swede Hollow, 52, 82
Swedish immigrants, 33, 52
Sweeny, Robert O., 20, 21, 94
Swiss, 21

T

Taliaferro, Lawrence, 6, 11
Taylor, David V., 85, 89, 97, 98
Taylor, Zachary, 10, 27
Temperance society, 28
The Appeal, 55
The Great American History Theatre, 97
The Helper, 76
The Migrant, 55
They Chose Minnesota, 79, 85, 97
Thompson, James, 9, 12, 21
Thursday Club, 71
Torre de San Miguel Homes, Inc., 99
Town Square, 91
Treaties of Traverse des Sioux and Mendota, 30
Tri-City Age, 71
Turner, Dr. Valdo, 77
Turpin, Mary, 29

Twin City Ordnance Plant, 88
Twin City Rapid Transit Company, 69
typhoid fever epidemic, 54-55

U

U.S.S. Ward, 87
Ullman, Amelia, 32, 39
Ullman, Joseph, 32
unemployment, 85
Union Hall, 78
United Charities, 63
United States Immigration Commission, 58
United States Sanitary Commission, 39
United States Supreme Court, 8, 67
United Way, 63
Upper and Lower Reservations, 30, 40, 41, 100
Upper Landing or levee, 13, 15, 29, 37, 50, 90
Upper Midwest Indian Center, 102

V

Valentine, Aldermen D. H., 38
Van Liew, Henry, 96
velocipede mania, 45
victory gardens, 60, 88
Vietnamese Alliance, 106
Vietnamese Buddhist Association of
    Minnesota, 106
Vietnamese Catholic Community, 106
Vietnamese Communists, 105
Vietnamese Cultural Association of
    Minnesota (VICAM), 106
Vietnamese League, 106

W

Wabasha Street bridge, 45
Wahpekute, 30
Wahpeton, 30
walking papers, 100
War Eagle, 37
War of 1812, 6, 10
war plants, 88, 98
Weber, Dr. Earl, 77
Welcome Hall, 78
West Seventh Street neighborhoods, 44, 48, 51
West Side, 32, 44, 48, 52, 58, 64, 68, 74, 78, 82,
    83, 87, 91, 98, 100, 105
West Side Story II, 64
Wheaton, J. Frank, 74
Whipple, Episcopal Bishop Henry B., 101
Whiting, Frank M., 95
Wigington, Clarence, 77
Wilkin, Alexander, 37
Wilkins, Roy, 75, 78
Williams, J. Fletcher, 11, 13, 14, 35

Williamson, Dr. Thomas, 28
Willius, Gustav, 31
Wilson, August, 97
Winter Carnival, 69
Woemet, Sharey Hesed, 49
Women's Civic League, 72
women's suffrage, 70
Works Progress Administration (WPA), 86
World Theatre, 96
World Trade Center, 26
World War I, 59, 60, 68, 70, 71, 81, 87, 100, 108
World War II, 68, 87, 88, 90, 92, 97, 99, 100, 104

Y
Yankees, 10, 52
YMCA, 68
Yoerg, Anthony, 32
YWCA, 60, 68

Z
Zuckerman, Pinchas, 94

PHOTO CREDITS

hotographs on the pages indicated are from the collection of the Minnesota Historical Society and are reprinted with their permission:

1, 2, 3, 4, 5, 6 - (T. R. Gettys), 8 - (Seth Eastman), 9, 10, 11, 12, 13, 14, 15, 16, 17 - (Andrew Frankensh), 19, 20, 21 - (Robert O. Sweeney), 22, 23 - (Zimmerman), 26, 27, 28, 29, 30, 31, 32 - (T. C. Healy), 33, 34, 35, 36, 37 - (Martin's Gallery), 38, 41 - (Fredericks), 42, 43, 44, 45, 46 - (St. Paul Book and Stationery), 47, 48 - (C. P. Gibson - Central Presbyterain Church), 50, 51, 52, 53 - (Flashlighters), 54, 56 - (Whitney), 59, 60, 61, 63 - (A. F. Raymond), 64, 65 - (ST. PAUL NEWS), 65 - (MINNEAPOLIS TRIBUNE), 66, 67, 70, 71, 72, 73, 74 - (C. P. Gibson), 75, 76, 77, 79, 80, 81, 82, 83, 84, 85, 86, 87, 88, 89,90, 91, 92, 93, 94, 95, 96 - (L. N. Scott collection), 97, 98 - (PIONEER PRESS), 99, 102, 103, 105, 107 - (Michael Kieger), 108.

Other photo credits include:
David Gonzales, p. 102.
GRAND GAZETTE/HIGHLAND VILLAGER, Mike Long, p. 104.
Minneapolis Institute of Art, p. 7.
THE CIRCLE, NATIVE CITY NEWS, Dale Kakkak, pgs. 100 -101.